Blessings from the Beach
Transformation at the Edge of the Sea

Mickey Eliason

Copyright 2017 by Mickey Eliason

ISBN:0692828907   Softcover version 978-0-6928-28890-9

All rights reserved. No part of this book may be reproduced or transmitted in any form or by any means, electronic or mechanical, including photocopying, recording, or by any information storage and retrieval system, without permission in writing from the copyright owner.

All photos were taken by Mickey Eliason and are copyright-protected.

Table of Contents

Acknowledgments/Gratitude..3
1. Finding Your Inner Beach Bum...4
2. Cultivating Beachwise Wisdom..12
3. Awakening to the Beach..23
4. Essence: Being Worth Your Salt...31
5. Flexibility, Fluidity and other "F" Words..39
6. Patience or Slowing to a Beach Rhythm..45
7. Peace and Love, Man..51
8. Reflection and Integration...58
9. Solitude..66
10. Cycles of Life..73
11. Change...82
12. Grounding and Connection...89
13. Fear: Tsunamis, Sharks, Pain, and Other Terrors 96
14. Wonder, Inspiration, and Joy..101
15. Protection, Resources, and Healing...108
16. Detachment: Letting Go..114
17. Clarity, Confusion, and Fog..119
18. Spaciousness and Timelessness..124
19. Balance...129
20. Boundaries, Borders, and Margins...136
21. Aquanimity..141
22. Beachwise As a Way of Life...145
Works Cited..151
Postscript: Using This Book in Discussion Groups........................154

Acknowledgments/Gratitude

No creative expression is conceived or born in isolation, and this book is no exception. So many people and places contributed to this book that I could not name them all. In essence, every person and situation of my life contributed to this moment, but a few people are notable for their significant influence at this particular point in my life. My teacher/mentor, Angeles Arrien, provided brilliant and pithy insights on life that inspired this book. I spent so much of my time on beaches reflecting on or writing about things that Angeles said, that I can hardly separate any wisdom that might be found here from what I learned directly from her. I am truly blessed to have had such a teacher. My deepest gratitude goes to fellow life travelers who sought to "walk a mystical path with practical feet" as Angeles so aptly put it, in the various groups that she organized over the years, and that have continued after her death. Thank you for sharing your experiences so we could all learn. All of you are in this book and in my heart.

I would not have had the courage to move across the country without a soul-mate/best-friend who offered the emotional, spiritual, and material support that made the move possible. She introduced me to new worldviews and opportunities that truly sparked my life transformation. Both her presence in my life during the critical two years of deciding whether to move and trying to adjust to the new living situation, and then her absence, have taught me valuable lessons. Other friends who patiently listened to me as I agonized over the stresses of moving and adjusting to a new life have been instrumental in maintaining my sanity.

My family has been a steady source of support and inspiration throughout my life. My parents and my siblings and their families are kind, gentle, and nurturing folks. My father Melvin, in particular, modeled a love of nature that inspired this work. Some of my fondest memories are of the family tramping through the woods with one of my younger siblings on his shoulders, and later in his life, of Dad puttering in his garden where he frequently grew certain vegetables for their sheer beauty even though no one in the family was fond of eating them. My mother, Nellie, supported me through the move across the country, although I knew she did not want me to live so far away. I tried to share my love of my new home with her to help her understand the appeal of living on the west coast. To all my family, thanks from the bottom of my heart.

1
Finding Your Inner Beach Bum

"Exultation is the going of an inland soul to sea." (Emily Dickinson)

    At some point in this journey of life on earth, many of us experience a feeling of restlessness or a longing for some deeper meaning in our lives and a need to find or return to our authentic selves. We seek to recapture the parts of ourselves that were stifled, buried, or frightened into a little corner of our souls. For many of us, the loss of self is related to our unnatural lives, lived out of rhythm with nature. One of the paths to regaining our lost selves and finding purpose and meaning in life is to reconnect with nature and get back into nature's rhythm.

    When an inexplicable longing and restlessness struck me around the time of my 50th birthday, I thought I was experiencing a unique personal problem, but I did not know how to label it. Was it a midlife crisis, depression, a spiritual crisis? I did not have the language to talk about it with my friends and family, so I let it fester inside of me for a number of months. Then I moved to the west coast and the restlessness dissipated quickly, carried away on an outgoing tide. I discovered the power of the beach as a wisdom teacher. All of the pieces began to fall into place, and I started to heal and grow into a more mature and grounded being.

This is not just the story of rediscovering my true self on the beach. Instead it is a human story of re-connecting our inner and outer natures. Most of us must do this at some point. I began to reconnect with nature and my inner self partly by reading widely from psychology texts, spiritual and wisdom teachings, and nature writing, and partly by seeking the help of a skilled teacher. But mostly the wisdom arose from my direct experience on the beach. I learned that my experience was far from unique. Most people, particularly adults in their second half of life, must learn similar lessons and come into their authentic selves, or they become bitter and unhappy with life.

I will share some of my experiences to illustrate the main points, but I hope that you will see yourself in these pages. If you have an inner beach bum, like me, you may resonate directly with some of my beach analogies and experiences. If your heart and soul lie in the mountains, the forest, the desert, the plains, or some other form of nature, what did you learn from your experiences with earth, rock, plant, trees, and fellow creatures? All of the earth is a sacred vessel for spiritual teaching and enhances our evolution as human beings. To open up a discussion of the beach as a crucible for personal growth and development, I will start with my own story.

My Journey to Beach Bum-dom

At 52 years of age, I moved from Iowa to the west coast and created an entirely new life for myself. After a half century of living in the land-locked rural Midwest, I made the transition from rippling waves of soybean and cornfields to ocean waves. I moved from a small town to a vibrant city. I left my stoic predominantly Scandinavian upbringing to live in the most multicultural city in the United States, where unique personal expression is encouraged rather than repressed. I went from a culture where emotions, both positive and negative, were suppressed in favor of the "stiff upper lip" approach to life, and where Californians were viewed with some suspicion, to a place where people are much more free to express their emotions and their identities. I moved to a location with many more diverse opportunities for personal growth and spiritual development. My Iowa weather-sense and experience of four distinct seasons, with hot humid summers and blistering cold winters, had to adapt to year-long mild temperatures and the vagaries of fog. For months my Iowa-conditioned brain could not figure out if the overcast signaled fog or impending rain. I was dumbfounded by the microclimates of San Francisco. How can it be raining on this hill and sunny less than a mile away?

At first, I was uncertain about my ability to make this move. I had never thought of myself as a city dweller. For years, I had traveled to various parts of the United States, but the only times that I really felt I could live somewhere else were during my infrequent visits to San Francisco. When visiting most cities, I was ready to come home after three days. The noise of city streets, the smog, the congestion of bodies, and the crowded-in feeling made me long for the peace and expansiveness of my home. I was not sure that I could actually leave my comfortable life in Iowa. I had a steady job that most of the time I liked (but did not love), a nice house with a beloved garden, a low crime neighborhood, lifelong friends, and most of my family to tie me to my home, my birth state. Why would I want to move to one of the most expensive cities in the country where I knew few people and had no job prospects? Could I cope with city traffic given that rush hour where I was living was more accurately described as "rush ten minutes?" But something had to change in my life. Recent experiences, beginning with losing my father, followed closely by a stressful, unfulfilling relationship, the death of my sister-in-law at a much too young age, and turning 50, had made me restless and searching for something more or something different in my life. I was burned out and in a spiritual crisis characterized by lack of meaning and purpose in my life. Then I met my soul mate. She lived in San Francisco, a place I had been considering as an option for over a year. So I took a leave of absence from my job and set up residence in San Francisco for three months to figure out if I could move across the country and become a city dweller.

On my many brief visits to San Francisco in the ten years before this trip, I had stayed in Union Square and explored the east side of the city; the bay side. I had trudged up and down the hills, gazed in wonder at the bay and the bridges, rode the cable cars, explored the alleys in Chinatown, and taken the ferry to Sausalito, but I had never made it to the ocean side of the city. On one day in June, about three weeks into my extended stay, I hopped on the N Judah train and rode to the end of the line. I noticed the difference the minute I got off the train. The air smelled different here and there was a sense of spaciousness and energy. It no longer felt, smelled, or sounded like a city. I could not yet see the ocean, but I felt my heart start to expand and my spirits soar. I had to climb a small ridge, cross a road, and pass between the sand dunes covered in ice plant. Suddenly, there it was, Ocean Beach. I wondered, why the lack of imagination in the name? Hadn't some early white male explorer planted his name on this beach like every other place? But I digress.

Ahead of me, stretching to the western horizon was the deep blue Pacific Ocean, spilling onto four miles of sandy beach in long rolling and breaking waves. The water was dotted with surfers, floating on their boards in their black wetsuits. To my right, the purple-tinged hills of the Marin Headlands and Mount Tam loomed in the distance. A huge cargo ship silently cruised into the mouth of the bay between San Francisco and Marin to eventually pass out-of-sight under the Golden Gate Bridge. I paused at the edge of the dunes to remove my shoes and socks. It was one of those rare warm and sunny days in June in San Francisco, although I did not yet know just how rare those days were. The sun reflected off the ocean like millions of tiny mirrors and the slow rolling breakers spilled over dramatically into a foaming white head of sea spray. The sound of crashing waves, gurgling backwash, and rattling stones dominated the soundscape.

I moved carefully down the beach toward the water, awkwardly slipping and sliding in the deep, dry shifting sand. I didn't yet have my "beach legs." Finally I reached the hard-packed damp sand nearer to the water's edge, and paused to roll up my pants legs. Then something extraordinary happened. A wave unexpectedly flowed up the sand to where I was standing, and that cold Pacific water enveloped my legs up to the knees, drenching the bottom of my blue jeans. As the water receded, sand oozed between my toes, the firm foundation giving way under me, literally and figuratively. At that off-balance moment, I felt as though a lightning bolt had struck me, and a moment of intense clarity washed over me like the wave. *"I'm home. This is where I'm meant to be."*

This baptism was the first of several "aha" moments that shaped my life over the next few years. That day on the beach, I knew I was moving to San Francisco, and the rest--finding a job, searching for affordable housing, packing, moving from the house where I had lived for more than 15 years, from the city where I had spent my entire adult life--were just the minor details. Over the next year, I sold my house and nearly everything in it, moving only a few clothes and books, a bag of river rocks, and a box full of photo albums. I left behind a life that had become too cluttered with material things…the house, the furniture, the garden, the wood shop, and all the accessories attached to a three-bedroom house. While I had derived much pleasure from these things earlier, now it felt important to scale down to the bare minimum and simplify my life. My life's purpose was not to be found in those things, but rather in a new way of being in the world. I also left behind the burned out old shell of a human being that I had become; cynical, sharp-tongued and pessimistic. I began to wake up.

I spent a year in transition, going between San Francisco and Iowa. For that first year, I lived mostly in the hippie village of Haight Ashbury. When I finally pinned down a couple of temporary jobs that could support me for a year, I started looking for more permanent housing. One day, on a tip from an acquaintance, I visited a 1920s Spanish style apartment building not too far from where I had my beach epiphany. The apartment manager first showed me an apartment on the second floor, overlooking a busy street. The apartment was quaint and appeared well-maintained. Then she said that there was another apartment available on the fourth floor. The minute I walked into that one, identical to the apartment on the second floor in all ways but one, I knew I was home. The difference was the view. The living room had a floor to ceiling window spanning six by six feet with a breath-taking view. The building sat on a hill, and this south-facing fourth floor apartment overlooked all of Ocean Beach, and in fact, the coastline for more than 10 miles. I signed the lease on the spot and moved in the next day. The beach became part of my daily life that very day and I began to learn about tides, currents, waves, and sand. Even today, sometimes I look out my window and think I'm on vacation. The lines between vacation and daily life have been blurred and I have learned so many lessons of work/play balance and daily time in nature as a result.

Over the next few years, I tried to learn what it all meant. Why was I called here? How was the beach implicated in my personal and spiritual maturation? Why did it feel like home? Would I ever grow tired of the beach? I explored my new surroundings, cruising up and down the coast, stopping at every beach along the way. I was amazed by the variety and unique character of each beach. Some had long, smooth, fine sandy shores, whereas others were dotted with huge boulders or were mostly littered with cobbles. Some had crumbly sandstone cliffs, some had granite boulders, and yet others had gentle berms covered in ice plant. There were protected coves and beaches exposed to the open sea. What they had in common was the ability to delight and inspire. I had to learn the sounds and sights of low tides and high tides, and became much more attuned to moon cycles.

I decorated my new studio apartment on the hill in rocks and shells and filled a vacuum cleaner bag with sand at least once a week. My car became a beach buggy filled with extra shoes, towels, rocks, shells, sand dollars, and of course, the ubiquitous sand. My cynicism was quickly replaced with a newfound wonder and awe for the beauty of my surroundings. Pessimism hung on longer as I stressed over finding a permanent job, but then was more slowly replaced with a renewed sense of purpose, even though at first I did not know what that purpose was. I had to trust that I was in the right location to find my rightful place in the world. My child-like curiosity was restored as I began to explore the diverse neighborhoods of the city and that sense of wonder and discovery hoisted me out of my rut.

I found a teacher/mentor for the first time in my adult life and joined a learning and healing community of like-minded souls working with her. We were all trying to better our relationships, improve our health, and foster positive growth. I soaked up books and CDs about transformational change and leading the meaningful life. I went to workshops, lectures, and dharma talks, and I walked labyrinths. And I processed all this new information on the beaches of the San Francisco Bay Area.

At first, the beach seemed a new, novel, and wondrous territory to explore, but I viewed it mainly as a place of recreation. I associated it with vacation or leisure. It felt like "home," but the deeper meanings of that sense of being home eluded me. It was not until after three years that the beach wisdom began to manifest. There was no sudden epiphany around this, but instead an insight that came after considerable reflection and integration. I slowly came to recognize the beach as a very special place or as Joan Anderson said in *A Walk at the Beach*, *"The beach is to me a sacred zone between the earth and sea, one of in-between places where transitions can be experienced—where endings are mourned and beginnings birthed"* (p. 2). I began to understand why the beach called so strongly at one of the most potent transition points of my life so far.

Then in October of 2008, I had another transformative moment. This third "aha" moment occurred just after I had finished the first of several year long personal growth programs called The FourFold Way, with powerful and inimical teacher/mentor Angeles Arrien. Near the end of this transformative experience, I had unpacked the one box from Iowa that was still on a shelf, found a battered copy of Anne Morrow Lindbergh's *Gift from the Sea*, and re-read it with new eyes. It had not made a great impression on me the first time I read it, but for some reason, I had kept the book for years. This second reading of the book sparked much deeper thinking and I could resonate with Lindbergh's thoughts about life at the beach as more than just a place of recreation. Then one Saturday morning a week after finishing the book, I went to a workshop where the leader guided us through an exercise about our purpose in life. She asked me and the other participants to generate very concrete goals that were compatible with that purpose. This was not a new activity for me. I had been contemplating my purpose for the past few years, and had come to realize that teaching was my primary calling. I started my list, and then a wave of an idea drenched me like that sneaker wave had a few years earlier. I had to write a book about my epiphany on the beach, a book that would integrate the experiences of the past several years, the things I have been learning about aging, taking risks, courage, authenticity, new beginnings, and finding myself on the beach. The book would be loosely modeled after *Gift from the Sea*, and supplemented with the pearls of knowledge and the wealth of skills I was learning from Angeles Arrien, and from my diverse reading and discussions with friends. This book would take my life purpose of teaching to a different audience, outside of the university, and would be written in a more heartfelt way than my previous books.

After the workshop, I drove to the nearest beach located in the beautiful Presidio, a greenbelt on the north end of San Francisco. Baker Beach, with its spectacular view of the iconic Golden Gate Bridge and the Marin headlands a mile across the strait, is my favorite urban beach getaway. I wrote a draft of this opening section in about ten minutes in a chill wind of the fall afternoon as a narrow band of fog was rolling in, right down the middle of the Golden Gate Strait. When I finished, I looked up. The fog now covered the tops of the two art deco towers, but it was still clear under the bridge. I could see that the sun was still shining beyond the bridge and white sailboats dotted the bay. A pair of dolphins cruised up and down the beach, delighting the few remaining beach revelers. Someone out of sight in the picnic area was drumming, the rhythmic human-made sound blended harmoniously with the rhythmic crashing of the waves. It was an auspicious start for a book, I thought, conceived there on that sandy strip of land. The rest of the book materialized in spits and spurts over the next few years as I continued to work with Angeles Arrien, and spend long chunks of time in solitude and silence on a deserted beach somewhere up or down the coast. I put the book aside for long periods of time; once for two years while my focus was on my mother's dying process, another transformative experience. Angeles had told me that the death of my father would set me on a search for meaning in life, and the death of my mother would set me on a soul's journey. That was certainly true. I started the book with a goal of finding meaning and purpose, and then it deepened into a soul exploration when I returned to it after my mother died.

Living a beach philosophy

The rest of this book explores what it means to live the "beachwise" life as Anne Morrow Lindbergh called it; a life that is fully engaged and awake. Each section integrates information about the beach or the ocean with wisdom teachings and each section ends with reflection questions to foster further development as a beach bum. Another valuable lesson I had learned from Angeles was the importance of working with deep questions, or as Rumi variously said, "love the questions," and "live the questions." So each chapter offers a range of questions—I don't intend for everyone to work with every question, but hopefully at least one question be relevant to your current situation and help you go deeper. Writing about tidal flats, John Hay (*In Defense of Nature*) observed:

> *"their volatility is open to our own, even those waves of emotion which may not fly loose over a sandbar, or be useful to investigation, but are of nature and her sea sure enough. They invite me to an extension of myself, with no divisions of matter or spirit."* (p. 61)

My hope for this book is to demonstrate the power of the beach to open us to that unity of matter and spirit, of Nature in the largest sense and nature in our unique personal sense. I do not pretend to have fully achieved beachwise wisdom myself. I believe it is a lifelong, ongoing process, but I have had glimpses of the ecstasy that accompanies embracing the beach as one of life's greatest teachers.

We all experience the trials and tribulations of life on earth, and must find ways to continue to grow, and to thrive in whatever situations we are thrown into. We all need to find our inner strength and reduce the toxic forces that plague our lives. We all have to deal with the noise, rush, and incessant clamor of consumer culture, the competitive marketplace in which many of us work, and all the distractions that seduce us away from living out our life dreams. Finding a sacred place where we can return to our true natures and put our lives in perspective can be a life-saver. For me, that place is the beach. Whatever your sacred place may be, I hope you will find inspiration in my musings on the lessons found on the sandy shore. This is not merely my story, but a sharing of my experience on the universal journey of humans from birth to death. We can turn on the automatic pilot and cruise through our lives like zombies, or we can wake up and maximize the limited time we have on this beautiful earth. The choice is ours. For myself, I choose the beach.

Going deeper
1. What does "home" mean to you? Do you feel at home where you currently live?
2. Do you have a story of homecoming that needs to be told?
3. What transitions are you living with now? This could be related to home in the sense of your work or creative endeavors, your relationships, your health, finances, or spiritual development.

2
Cultivating Beachwise Wisdom

"The beach is not a place to work; to read, write, or think...then some morning in the second week, the mind wakes, comes to life again. Not in a city sense—no—but beachwise."
(Anne Morrow Lindbergh, Gift from the Sea, p. 15)

More than sixty years ago, Anne Morrow Lindbergh began her book with these insightful words. Lindbergh was writing about profound insights stimulated by a short vacation on the beach, but what about those of us who make the beach our backyards, who return to the shore repeatedly? What does it mean to make the beach a way of life? For many of us, the beach becomes "the" place for the real work of life; the deep reflection about our life purpose and dreams, the integration of our experiences, and the pondering about how to keep growing. The beach is one of many places that encourage the mind to "wake up" so we can see the world as it really is, not as our minds have constructed or wished it to be, and the place where integration work can happen, so we learn from our experiences rather than repeat our mistakes.

We humans tend to understand the world around us through metaphor, a word from the Latin that means carry (pherein) beyond (meta). I believe that the beach and the ocean beyond it are powerful metaphors for our everyday lives. We speak of being "swept away" or "waves of emotion" overtaking us, of being "between the devil and the deep blue sea" and describe the ebb and flow of our lives as if they were tides. When big events transform our way of thinking, we describe them as a "sea change." When we are confused and thoughts are in a muddle, we say we are in "a fog," and when we are beginning a new endeavor, we "set sail on a new course." When someone keeps us steady in our lives, we refer to them as "anchors." When we are communicating well with another person, we say that we are "on the same wavelength."

When we are overburdened and stressed at work, we say we are "drowning in paperwork," and when all is going well, it is going "swimmingly." A wise person is said to have "depth" whereas the irritable one is "crabby." We surf the internet or TV channels, leave our shells when we emerge into the social world, and fish for information. When we need deeper understanding of something, we "plumb the depths." If we are unable to understand, we "cannot fathom" the problem. Good things arrive to us in our "ship of fortune" and when things are going poorly, we refer to them as "wrack and ruin." The beach is with us in our everyday language, whether we are conscious of it or not.

In fact, the waves at the beach represent a universal force. As Susan Casey (*The Wave: In pursuit of the rogues, freaks, and giants*) noted, *"Waves are the original primordial force. Anywhere there's energy in motion, there are waves, from the farthest corners of the universe down to the cells in your eyeball…waves are a majestic demonstration of the unseen force that powers everything."* No wonder we are drawn to the beach, one of the places where this power can be seen directly.

Writers and the Beach

"There is no frigate like a book to take us lands away." (Emily Dickinson)

Many writers have turned to the sea for inspiration, and have written novels, poems, and/or autobiographical accounts of the power of the sea to effect transformative life change. I have found kindred spirits in their writing, in these books that combined my love of the beach with a zest for learning, reading, and writing. Jennifer Ackerman (*Notes from the Shore*) noted, *"I discovered in nature the same appeal I found in books. Both were engrossing, filled with the richness of particularities and yet mysteriously universal. Both were the stuff of perspective."* (p. 18)

I, too, find that the beach is a great place to integrate book learning with deeper inner knowing, and to figure out how to put new learning into practice. Reading followed by beach walking engages both the intellect and the senses, integrating the information first assembled in my head throughout my body. If I walk on the beach while mulling over ideas I read, that learning can be embodied rather than just stored in some corner of the brain. It is a much deeper level of learning and understanding than the pure intellectual level. As Ackerman said, it provides perspective.

Joan Anderson, in *A Year by the Sea*, relates the story of finding herself through a year of solitary living on Cape Cod. She learned how to make that critical shift from defining herself through her family to forging her own unique natural self. It was solitude in nature, by the sea, that helped her to find her true self and find new meaning in life. In a later book, *A Walk on the Beach*, she began,

> *"Not a day goes by that I don't take a walk on the beach. The beach is truly home, its broad expanse of sand as welcoming as a mother's open arms. What's more, this landscape, which extends as far as the eye can see, always reminds me of possibility. It is here I can listen to my inner voice, shed inhibitions, move to the rhythm of the waves, and ask the universe unanswerable questions…There is no more doubt that the sea is in my veins than that there is sand in my shoes."* (p. 1)

I felt akin to Joan Anderson in many ways. She went to the ocean to find herself. One day in a dense fog on the beach, she found an incredible mentor, Joan Erikson, then a 90 year-old woman who was wife and life companion to famous psychologist Erik Erikson. Joan Erikson was a formidable intellect and personality herself, although she never received the acclaim that her husband did. I moved to the ocean to find myself in a literal and figurative fog about the direction my life should take, and I, too, found mentors who provided the guidance I needed to navigate the storm of my midlife crisis.

Some authors write about the sea or the beach from a seemingly more scientific perspective, like marine biologist Rachel Carson. Although she is most well known for jumpstarting the ecology movement with her book about the dangers of pesticides, *The Silent Spring*, her greatest love was the ocean. Her books were meant to educate the public about the shore, ocean life, and our place in it, but they can be read as love letters to the ocean. A reviewer from Time magazine described *The Edge of the Sea* as "*catching the life breath of science on the still glass of poetry.*" Rachel Carson's books literally took my breath away at times and more than once, brought tears to my eyes. You will find many quotes from her profound love of the sea in this book.

Another naturalist, Mary Parker Buckles, in *Margins,* shared her experiences of moving to the Long Island Sound. She grew up an "inlander," like me, and as an adult found joy living by and learning from the sea. Some of her comments really resonated with me. For example, she described her first year of living by the sea this way: *"I spent most of 1989 touching my new environment as if it were a cake about to rise. When I tested its texture against that of my previous life, I found it pushed back at me in ways no other place had"* (p. ix).

Her book is divided into the four elements that make up the margins of her world: Land, water, intertidal space, and air. Those elements are powerful teachers about our life experiences, and I could viscerally relate to her metaphor. The beach had certainly "pushed back at me" in a powerful way. I was also inspired by many other writers who were passionate about ecology and treating the earth as a sacred home to our physical bodies, and have mined their jewels of wisdom to decorate the pages of this book.

Other authors explore the beach or the ocean from an artistic, aesthetic, and/or spiritual viewpoint. Andy Goldsworthy makes art from found objects in nature—some of the most dramatic are the elaborate stone sculptures he creates at low tide, so that the beautiful creation is dismantled by the incoming tide. His work reminds me that all beauty is transitory and fleeting, so we must enjoy it when we encounter it, and be grateful we had the experience to witness it after its gone. Gary Greenberg takes microphotographs of sand from beaches around the world, finding incredible diversity, color, and texture to what most of us perceive as uniform, beige sand. Gideon Bosker and Lena Lencek, in *Beaches*, collected photographs that they thought captured the essence and diversity of the world's seashores. I loved the opening words of their book:

> *"What American reared on the childhood classic The Wizard of Oz can't relate to Dorothy's magical mantra, 'There's no place like home'? Well, we have a confession to make. Beach bums from infancy, we were always skeptical about the strength of Dorothy's longing for the flat fields of Kansas, because for us, there could only be one place with the power to rock the soul and feed the heart—and that place was, and continues to be, the beach. On this unstable and dangerously seductive strip of land, the alluring alchemy of water, sand, wind, and light evokes in us sensations that collapse past, present, and future, sex and death, the sacred and the unholy, into a single, glorious experience of pleasure." (p. 11)*

I may not have been a beach bum from infancy (at least on the conscious level), but I gave up my Dorothy-like homeland on the plains to reclaim my inner beach bum. My story is the reverse of Dorothy and Toto's journey in many ways. I had to leave my lifelong home on the plains to find myself. I found home in a new landscape, not the comforts of my former home.

I found Bosker and Lencek's beautiful book in the gift shop at Sea Ranch, a spectacular planned community on ten miles of northern California's rugged, rocky shoreline. I wrote these words as I gazed at the ocean from the loft of a vacation rental home, and the sea roared at high tide from the open window next to the desk. That day, I felt the timelessness and power of the sea. It was not peaceful at that moment, but charged with energy, insistent that I think more deeply about issues. In other words, I felt inspired and energized. I have come to recognize that for me, low tides are often associated with reflection and contemplation, and high tides with creativity and energy.

Keats, Shelley, Byron, and other poets went to the sea for inspiration. The sea sparked books about transformation, survival, and perseverance, like The Old Man and the Sea, and Moby Dick. In ancient as well as contemporary times, the sea has inspired musicians. Who among us have not been touched by music, with its power to evoke emotions and memories?

> *"Sittin' here in limbo, waiting for the tide to flow" (Jimmy Cliff)*
> *"Sittin' on a dock of the bay, watching the tide roll away" (Otis Redding)*
> *"And so castles made of sand fall into the sea eventually" (Jimi Hendrix)*
> *"Catch a wave and you're riding on top of the world" (Beach Boys)*
> *"First the tide rushes in plants a kiss on the shore then rolls out to sea and the sea is very still once more" (Righteous Brothers)*

Finally, there are the ancient and contemporary wisdom teachers who urge us to reconnect with nature in order to grow and evolve as human beings. I draw heavily from the work of Angeles Arrien here, as my primary teacher/mentor for several years. As a cultural anthropologist, she culled her wisdom from years of study of indigenous cultures around the world, synthesizing universal truths about human communication and connection. Angeles was one of those profound truth-tellers with a unique gift of conveying wisdom to her mentees in exactly the way they needed to hear it, at exactly the time they most needed it. I appreciate that she so often rooted her wisdom in nature practices and/or stories. Her passing in 2014 affected me profoundly, but she continues to be my primary teacher as I mull over the lessons I learned from her.

Many wisdom teachers use nature metaphors or suggest practices to help us reconnect with nature; these too, have inspired this work. Some, like Bill Plotkin (*Nature and Human Development*) suggested that we must mature as individuals and as a species. He proposed that our society is arrested at a pathological adolescent stage of egocentrism, and that only growth into mature adulthood will save us and the earth and seas. That growth, he suggested, comes from a blending of nature and culture. I wondered how we had become so alienated from nature, and when we lost ourselves as a human species. Obviously, it started a long time ago, but it is not too late to reconnect with nature.

The History of the Beach

"There is a pleasure in the pathless woods. There is a rapture on the lonely shore." (Lord Byron)

As I began to explore my new relationship to the beach, and to the ocean beyond it, I needed a broader perspective to ground my experience. Finding inspiration or ecstasy at the beach has a long history, and I yearned to understand how the beach had affected others before me, so that I could better comprehend my own experience. Books by marine biologists, activists, conservationists, and other scientists provided a starting point for the physical and material history of the beach, but did not provide the whole story. Lena Lencek and Gordon Bosker (*The Beach: A History of Paradise on Earth*) summarized the social and cultural history and that provided the historical perspective I was looking for. My experience of finding myself at the beach was mirrored by countless other lost souls throughout time, although the interpretations of our experiences are tempered by contemporary understandings of science, religion, spirituality, and culture. I distill some of Lencek and Bosker's lovely book here.

They proposed that beaches could not become the place of recreation and rejuvenation that they are now until two events had occurred. First, humankind had to become alienated from nature, and secondly, they had to have leisure time. Therefore, it was not until the growth of cities and industry produced urban life and an upper class that the beach took on a new modern meaning. Prior to this time, the sea and the beach were sites of daily living and struggles for survival for those who dwelled near the sea. Creation myths and stories of sea monsters or unpredictable and powerful gods and goddesses of the sea proliferated. The rise of the Roman Empire created the necessary conditions for a wealthy citizen class who had the resources to build villas by the sea and retreat to the beach to think, write, and rejuvenate their spirits.

After the collapse of the Roman Empire around 470 CE, the beach resort disappeared for the next millennium because of the rise of Christianity, with its denouncement of bodily pleasures so celebrated by the Romans, and by the movement of capitals inland and northward. In the Christian Bible, Eden has no sea, and many biblical passages depict the ocean as a terrifying place to be, where retribution, dangerous floods, and threat of being swallowed by whales warned people away from the sea. As Lencek and

Bosker noted, to the early Christians *"the beach is a line drawn in the sand beyond which the human mind should not venture; like all sacred thresholds, it could only be approached with great trepidation"* (p. 42). At the same time, plagues erupted throughout Europe, and bathing was thought to increase vulnerability to illness. It would not be until the mid 1600s that doctors began to recognize the curative value of bathing, especially submersion in mineral and salt water.

The view of the beach as a place of spiritual retreat was re-born in Great Britain, fostered by the Brits exploration of more exotic and warmer shores around the world, a fascination with Dutch seascape paintings, and a new appreciation of all things Roman. British tourists began to visit the seaside in Holland, Italy, and other warmer climes. The writing about the ocean at this time was related to the "sublime" experience of the sea—a mixture of terror and awe. For example, Edmund Burke in 1757 (*On the Sublime and Beautiful*) wrote, *"A level plain of a vast extent on land [can never] fill the mind with anything so great as the ocean itself… [it] produces a sort of delightful horror, a sort of tranquility tinged with terror."*

This terror of the ocean slowly diminished as physicians touted the medicinal benefits of sea bathing, and Bath, Great Britain became one of the first modern seaside resorts with its hot springs, Roman ruins and its proximity to London. Hearty Brits were subjected to traumatic immersions in the chilly water, plunged into and held under water by brawny "dippers" because the shock was thought to *"revitalize the organism, soothe anxieties, and help restore harmony between body and soul"* (p. 71). It was a combination of penance and therapy, highly compatible with British morals and disposition toward the body.

By the early 1800s, British romantic writers such as Byron, Wordsworth, Coleridge, Keats, Shelley, and Swinburne, were flocking to the ocean, not for the baths, but for reflection and self-discovery. The spiritual quest at the ocean was popularized. Along with the sea resort physician and their medicinal baths we could now find artists with their creative fire, and this era launched the solitary beach walker reveling in the senses and seeking enlightenment. Apparently, Shelley so languished when away from the sea that he had to periodically plunge his head into a basin of water to revive his spirits. Ironically, he drowned in the Ligurian Sea while sailing. The romantics also spawned an interest in swimming as a way to open up the bodily senses and learn about one's self at a deeper, primal level. Social elites of the time used the ocean as a metaphor for emotional experience and eroticism.

The advent of rail travel in Europe and the United States in the late 1800s plus the establishment of fixed holidays opened the seaside resort to the commoner, looking not only for spiritual release or healing, but escape and fun. A whole new era of the beach was launched, although many continued to flock to the beach for spiritual rejuvenation as well. Today the beach is shared by all social classes and includes sunbathers, surfers, dog walkers, volleyball players, beachcombers, and the soul searching for enlightenment, sometimes all rolled up in one person.

Accessing Beach Wisdom

"The shore is no dumb, immovable thing, but has a life and a wisdom of its own." (Jennifer Ackerman, Notes from the Shore, p. 26)

Both writers and non-writers alike seek deeper understandings about life from the narrow strip of sand between earth and sea. The beach can be a place of social gathering and pure fun, but as a tool for reflection and integration, it is best experienced in solitude. Beachwise philosophers haunt the urban beaches at 6 am, seeking that solitude, or travel off the beaten path to find the deserted beach. We are the ones at first resentful when beach revelers take over our beach, but then grudgingly, and finally, gleefully share the joy amidst the picnics, kites, and splashing children and dogs. But we most cherish the deserted beaches where we can be alone in nature, to foster the solitude needed for integrating our life experiences.

As Anne Morrow Lindbergh noted, the beach may not be the best place to "read, write, and think" in the usual way we think of these activities, but it is certainly a superb place to feel and to be. To truly transform and transcend our cultural brainwashing, we need to find a different way to experience life. Sitting in front of a TV or computer screen exposes us to countless messages of greed, desire, speed, and violence. We get distorted messages about our relationships and about gender, race, class, religious, and other roles or identities. We are distracted by work demands, no longer limited to the 9-5 office, because the demands are there on our multiple screens 24/7. We are addicted to email, instant messaging, tweeting, and checking our Facebook or Instagram pages, all superficial forms of dis-embodied communications that keep us stuck in the shallower parts of the mind. But when we go to the beach, the ocean's roar and the regular spilling over of the waves demand our attention. Sitting or walking by the ocean slows us down to nature's rhythm, and allows us to access a deeper part of ourselves than we typically use in our daily lives.

Beachwise thoughts and feelings may not lead to fully formed articulate sentences, but rather, to "aha" moments and deep insights to be put into words later. Thoughts originating at the beach may be experienced as a shift in perception or the sensations of contentment or bliss that are not easily rendered into words, but affect the way we live our lives. The surface thoughts of every day annoyances and the daily routines are washed away by the sea breezes, opening a space for deeper thoughts to arise. The beachwise philosophers sit in the sand dunes partially hidden in the tufts of dune grass, and they leave fresh footprints in the wet sand as they stroll in walking meditation. For many of us, the beach is the crucible for spiritual learning, for gaining insight about aging, forgiveness and letting go, and for reclaiming our sense of childlike wonder and playfulness. We wait for our "gift from the sea" and we are always rewarded with those gifts.

The beach gives us many blessings, but in return, we must extend our gifts and talents to the sea to honor the blessings. Angeles Arrien, in her introduction to *The Four-Fold Way*, noted:

> *"our word ecology comes from the Greek oikos, which means 'house.' As we move into the twenty-first century, it is the work of all human beings to attend to the health of both our 'inner' and 'outer' houses; the inner house of our selves, the limitless world within, and the outer house of the world in which we live our daily lives. Many people in contemporary society feel little or no connection between these two worlds."* (p. 3)

Wisdom teachings from around the world and in any historical time period urge us to reconnect our inner and outer worlds. In other words, we need Nature to connect to our own unique nature. Isn't it interesting that we describe our unique essence or usual way of being as our nature or being "natural?" Our language reveals the connection between the inner and outer worlds even if we have forgotten that link. We are corrupting our nature when we wrongly label our high tech, fast-paced lives spent mostly indoors, viewing nature only on a TV screen, as "natural." I am not proposing that we have to give up the advances of culture and technology, and try to turn back time, but I am suggesting that valuing the products of modern western culture and technology over the processes of nature have gotten us into a lot of trouble. It is time that we become more conscious about how we blend nature and culture in our daily lives. By extension, we must become part of a cultural movement to save the earth and the seas by taking political action and by educating others.

Mark Coleman, in *Awake in the Wild*, pointed out that wisdom teachings are full of inspiration and metaphors from nature; from forests, deserts, beaches, and mountain caves, and he offers meditations that enhance our connection with nature. I cite some of these later in the book. Coleman reminds us that nature is a place to get in touch with silence, stillness, and solitude; qualities that are rare in our fast-paced world. We have different relationships with different types of nature—some of us are drawn to the mountains, the thin air and expansive vistas exhilarate us or the rocky peaks give us a sense of awe. We get the "big picture" when we view the world from the top of a mountain peak, and our problems look small in comparison. The high places are a metaphor for perspective. We can see the "lay of the land" when we get up above our daily lives. When we are down in it, we are too close to see it clearly.

Some of us favor the calm waters of an alpine lake, or a babbling brook. Others favor the desert with its stark, spare beauty and some are drawn to the deep green forests, the tangled foliage of jungles, the abundant wildlife of riverbanks, or the broad spacious plains of rippling grasses. I believe there are different types of wisdom to be gained from these experiences. In our ancient wisdom/spiritual traditions, Jesus went to the desert, Moses and Mohamed went to the mountaintop, the Buddha to the forest, and indigenous peoples of many continents went on vision quests in the wilderness or mountains to gain understanding or to mature into adulthood. But nature can be experienced in small doses, in many different types of settings. We do not have to fast for 40 days in the desert to achieve benefits from nature. Even brief encounters with nature can help us to reconnect with our deeper selves and with the larger world outside of ourselves. We can learn much from how we respond to different types of nature experiences, as they give us clues about our deeper natures.

I grew up on the plains, where thunderclouds tumble in from the west. Weather does not change suddenly on the plains—you can see it coming miles off in the distance. Just before the storm hits, the air becomes noticeably charged. You can actually feel the electricity in the air; it makes the hair on your arms stand on end. Black clouds billow in the wind and blot out the sun, and hints of the downpour to come arrive in mists carried on the wind gusts. The sky rumbles ominously with thunder, muted at first, becoming deafening cracks and "booms" as the storm moves overhead. Distant lightning can illuminate the sky in jagged strikes that sear the earth, or in brilliant flashes in the upper atmosphere. After the storm passes, the air smells clean and fresh and the world sparkles like a jewel. There is nothing else quite like the drama of a Midwestern thunderstorm for conveying the raw energy and power of nature. A thunderstorm is certainly not a contemplative experience, but rather, it can be felt as an embodiment of power and the transformation of energy.

The lessons of the thunderstorm are quite different from the lessons of the quiet beach at sunset or the winter storm at sea. The forest at dusk has a very different feel than the starry skies of the desert at night. Our various experiences in nature may illuminate the variety of responses we have to daily life experiences as well, and how we react to the situations (our nature). The same lightning storm that thrilled and invigorated me, terrified my friend. She preferred to ride out the storm huddled in the basement with a flashlight at hand, whimpering in fear at each crack of thunder. I preferred to view the oncoming storm from a hilltop, waiting until the last possible minute before the downpour before coming indoors. I felt exhilarated and alive, a trait I got from my storm-chaser father who loved to be out in the midst of the storm. My friend grew up in a family that cowered in the basement. I tend to stay calm, even exhilarated during moments of stress; she tends to shut down. These are learned experiences to some extent, and can be changed with our consistent attention, but they partly reflect our core personality traits as well, and our responses to nature can be instructive in identifying those traits. Sometimes we cannot learn the lessons of the land that nourished us in childhood until we move away or visit other landscapes.

Now I live on the sunset coast, and find myself drawn to the beach to watch the blazing red-orange ball of sun sink slowly out of sight, and to sometimes be rewarded with the "green flash." The warm glow intensifies into deep reds and oranges, and lingers as a duller pink hue for several minutes after the sun disappears. Watching the sun set over the ocean is one of those rare experiences when we can directly witness the passage of time and honor the closing of another day. It has become a time to reflect on the day, rather than merely forget the opportunities to learn that the day presented.

As you think about your own experiences, pay attention to the responses you have had to different aspects of nature, or even differences in how nature speaks to you in different seasons, or different times of the day, or different light. The dynamic changes of nature reflect our own constantly changing emotional responses to the world around us.

Coming Home to the Beach

"Shall I part my hair behind? Do I dare eat a peach? I shall wear white flannel trousers and walk upon the beach." (T.S. Elliott, The Love Song of J. Alfred Prufrock)

I have come to learn that I feel most at home in my own skin when I am walking along a beach, listening to the long rolling waves that crash with a resounding BOOM. I have learned that peace and joy come from engaging all the outer senses: planting my bare feet in the wet sand, tasting the salty spray on my face, skin tingling from the ocean breezes, hearing the crash of the waves and the gurgle of the backwash, and smelling the salty tang of seaweed. If I look beyond the cresting waves to the endless horizon of water, I am looking beyond the known world and my perspective broadens. When all the outer senses are engaged fully at once, then the inner world can also come to life, and deeper insights rise and fall like the oncoming waves.

Rachel Carson, another incredible teacher of life through her writing about the ocean, expressed the connection many of us feel to the sea in this way.

> *"When we go down to the low-tide line, we enter a world as old as the earth itself—the primeval meeting place of the elements of earth and water, a place of compromise and conflict and eternal change. For us as living creatures it has special meaning as an area in or near which some entity that could be distinguished as life first drifted in shallow waters—reproducing, evolving, yielding that endlessly varied stream of living things that has surged through time and space to occupy the earth."*
> (The Edge of the Sea, p. xii-xiv)

The beach is our birthplace, and a constant source of creative inspiration and nurturing if we are only open to it. I realized years after my epiphany on the beach that the sense of coming home came from a deep realization that I had found my metaphorical birthplace. As the ultimate matriarchal elder, the ocean holds deep wisdom and nurturance for me, and for all who are open to receive it.

This book explores that concept of the beach as the place of learning about life from our maternal ancestor's knee. Pablo Neruda spoke of *"the university of the waves"* whereas others describe the edge of the sea as a place of worship, or the ocean as wise elder—grandmother ocean or father sea. Life's journey as a human being mimics the evolution of the earth's beaches, the cycles of life and death of waves, and the shifting changing sand. Our fate, along with all other creatures in the sea and on the earth, depends on our gaining wisdom from nature. I propose that wisdom can be gained from living life from a "beachwise" perspective. In this book, I draw from teachings from many different sources, but with a particular grounding in Anne Morrow Lindbergh's beautiful book, *Gift from the Sea*. Written sixty years ago, her reflections are as relevant today as they were then. Near the end of her book, Lindbergh summarized her "island precepts" or if I may rephrase, "beachwise wisdom" as containing the elements of *"simplicity, balance of physical, intellectual, and spiritual work; work without pressure; space for beauty and meaning; closeness to nature; life of the spirit, creativity, and relationships"* (p. 120).

These grains of sandy wisdom, and many others, are explored here. Each section that follows contains some thoughts about common life experiences, human traits, or feelings. The book is not an in-depth academic discourse, but rather mimics the type of thoughts or musings that come from walking on the beach. I hope that they may stimulate deeper reflections about the beach as a spiritual teacher.

I believe that a beachwise life practice runs deeper than Anne Morrow Lindbergh's book goes, far beyond the contemplation of our inner lives and our relationships. As Angeles Arrien so wisely pointed out, true beach wisdom involves an integration of our inner and outer worlds. We cannot survive and thrive as individuals unless we take responsibility for the grievous harm we as human citizens of the world have inflicted on our earth and sea, and we must find ways to live in harmony with the world, our home. As W.H. Auden once said, *"Thousands have lived without love, but not one without water."* All the self-knowledge and understanding in the world is nothing if we have no planet to support our lives.

Going Deeper
1. Think back on your past experiences at the beach. Have you received "gifts from the sea?" What have those gifts meant to you?
2. Find a quiet spot to sit or lie down for ten minutes. Visualize yourself at a beach—one you know well or one you imagine as your ideal beach-- and engage all your senses. Feel the sand beneath your feet—is it dry, wet, sharp, warm or cool? Taste and smell the salty air and pungent scent of seaweed, hear the birds and the surf, picture the ocean endlessly rolling out of sight on the horizon. And then focus on the very edge, with water surging, foaming, and receding in regular, yet unpredictable patterns. What feelings or thoughts arise when you fully engage your senses in this way?
3. Think about the different experiences you have had in nature. What types of geography are you most drawn to and why? What elements within the geography are you most drawn to—mountains, valleys, trees, rivers, sky? What lessons have geography or nature's elements taught you about life?
4. How about seasons? Do you feel more alive and energized by certain seasons? Do you hibernate in winter, going inward for reflection? Do you come alive in spring? What is your favorite season and why?

3
Awakening

The breeze at dawn has secrets to tell you.
Don't go back to sleep.
You must ask for what you really want.
Don't go back to sleep.
People are going back and forth across the doorsill
where the two worlds touch.
The door is round and open.
Don't go back to sleep. (Rumi)

    The beach, the threshold between land and sea, is one of the most powerful doorsills, or transitional places where two worlds touch. My awakening occurred at the beach, and I am committed to stay awake. In the western world, we often sleepwalk through our lives, engrossed by the stories of the past, re-living our moments of glory or rehashing the traumas, or we obsessively worry about the future, imagining the worst-case scenarios. Beachwise wisdom requires a commitment to being fully present and paying attention to each new moment. Going to the beach, but thinking only of that nagging problem at work, or fretting over a relationship problem and not seeing or feeling the ocean breezes, the warm sun, the grainy sand between the toes, is to lose an opportunity to access beach wisdom. As Thoreau put this idea: *"I feel a little alarmed when it happens that I have walked a mile into the woods bodily, without getting there in spirit…What business have I in the woods if I am thinking of something outside the woods?"* (*Writing Nature: Henry Thoreau's Journal*).

I feel the same way on the beach. Fortunately, there are steps we can take to wake up and stay awake. We can begin to recognize the things that put us to sleep. For me, they include indulging in the regrets of the past, lapsing into daydreams that create a false self-system or an unlikely fantasy future, watching too much television, or getting hooked on playing mindless computer games. Going to the beach can take me away from those temptations to go back to sleep, and bring me fully into the present moment where life is actually being lived.

Quieting the Mind

"Silence is an ocean. Speech is a river. When the ocean is searching for you, don't walk to the language-river. Listen to the ocean and bring your talky business to an end." (*Rumi*)

To access the deeper wisdom to be had from the beach, we must be open to see, hear, taste, touch, and in every way connect with the beach. That sensory awareness opens us to the creative problem solving we need to fix that problem at work or repair that damaged relationship later, when we go home. In contemporary western society, much has been written about mindfulness, and many people are learning mindfulness skills to improve their health. I applaud the efforts of many individuals to introduce mindfulness to the west (John Kabat-Zinn, Jack Kornfield and many others), and to teach people skills in paying attention, to waking up. However, some of what is taught today as mindfulness meditation by less knowledgeable teachers plays into the western tendency to separate mind and body, and seems to propose that we can control our bodies via the mind. My first exposure to mindfulness meditation was from a western psychologist who turned it into cognitive therapy, all about mind over matter and controlling one's thoughts. We did more talking than meditating. True mindfulness is not a practice in controlling, manipulating, or analyzing our thoughts, dreams, feelings, insights or our bodies, or merely changing our thoughts. Those ideas buy into the western notion of a separate mind and body.

Mindfulness, to me, is paying attention in a nonjudgmental way, without trying to change, control or manipulate. It acknowledges all the senses as well as the thoughts. It is an integration of mind and body that opens up access to some deeper part of our selves. I struggled for several years to develop a mindfulness practice on a meditation cushion indoors, with only modest results. Eventually I realized that I was trying to achieve some altered state of consciousness through thought alone. I only opened to a deeper meditative state when I planted my feet in the sand and drew a salty breath in and out. Being in nature engaged much more than just my mind. The beach activated the senses, perceptions, emotions, thoughts, and that indescribable something deep inside that I will call spirit for lack of a better word. Instead of using the word mindfulness, which is only one component of the experience, and stresses the western emphasis on mind, I think of this bigger process as awakening. It starts with activation of all the thoughts, feelings, and bodily sensations so that we become aware of them. Ultimately, I'd like to be more "mindless," and use my other faculties more often. As an academic, I spent many years cultivating the mind and being rewarded for writing that is devoid of feelings and sensory experiences. For nearly twenty years, I spent most of the hours of my workday, which was typically at least 10 hours long, in the "life of the mind." But as I started to shift into longer periods of engaging my body, feelings, and sensory experiences with more "mindlessness," the quality of my work improved. I was better able to discern what was important and discard the irrelevant distractions.

We are so accustomed to constant thought that we are often not aware of thinking. Mark Coleman (*Awake in the Wild*) noted that each person, on average, has about one thought per second, or about 84,000 thoughts per day. That is about the same number of resting heartbeats that we experience in a day. We tend to take in a minimal amount of sensory information before we jump to thoughts, and start making assumptions, judgments, comparisons, and conclusions. We do this in nature as well, reducing our capacity to really experience nature on a deeper visceral, sensory, and sensual way. Mindfulness meditation is about training the mind to be present to the moment we are experiencing--the Buddha said, *"the mind well trained brings ease."* But mind training is only one step to awakening the mind, body, and spirit to deeper experience; it is only one of many practices to cultivate wisdom. This mind training is about reminding ourselves to gather more sensory information—to suspend production of thought or judgment until a later time. If we focus on waves which break on average about every five seconds, and our breath which rises and falls along with the waves, perhaps we can slow down our thoughts accordingly, giving ourselves space between thoughts (or waves or breath) for deeper wisdom to surface. It's a skill we can learn at the beach and then transfer to our everyday life. I can imagine the waves breaking and synchronize my breathing for one minute at my desk and re-balance myself.

To experience a beachwise awakening, we must go to the beach with an open mind and heart. Anticipate wondrous things without expectations for the form that they will take. The beach is never mundane or dull, but neither is our daily life if we stay present to it. When did we fall into the trap of thinking our lives are routine and boring? Prior to moving to the west coast, my life had become automated. I had the same job, performed the same tasks repeatedly, went to the same restaurants, and lived in the same town for over 30 years. The only things that changed were my partners. I cycled through five relationships in 20 years. I realize now that I created this sense of dullness and routine by going to sleep and turning on the automatic pilot. My mind was focused on work or cycling between the past and the future, and I was ignoring my present life. I was living in my mind and not paying attention to my body, except for when I felt physical pain. I did not leave space for feeling my feelings, but instead made the leap to analyzing them immediately. I made no effort toward stepping out of the rut that I dug for myself. No wonder I could not sustain a relationship when I was not really awake. Relationships are lived in the present moment.

In reality, every day is unique and holds opportunities for growth and for wonder, for powerful connections with others, for deep insights, and for joy. This awareness can be fostered on the beach with its ever changing tides and shifting sands, with the occasional head popping out of the water, whiskers a-twitter as the seal watches with curiosity. Or maybe today I will be rewarded with the sight of a dolphin leaping from the water, a crab scuttling under a rock, or I will find the most beautiful smooth richly colored stone ever. If I am lucky, today my entire worldview may shift, dramatically altering the course of my life. But it can only happen if I am awake enough to recognize it. As the poet, Juan Ramon Jimenez noted, big changes can be happening without my conscious awareness:

> *My boat struck something deep;*
> *nothing happened*
> *Waves, water, silence*
> *Nothing happened?*
> *Perhaps everything has happened*
> *and I'm standing in the middle*
> *of my new life.*

How many opportunities did I miss because I was not paying attention? I became the person I am without recognizing what happened to me, because I was not awake.

Engaging the Senses

"Our camp grove fills and thrills with glorious light. Everything awakening, alert, and joyful…every pulse beats high, every cell life rejoices, the very rocks seem to thrill with life."
(John Muir, In Chris Highland, Meditations of John Muir)

Many nature writers have captured the sense of awakening that one often feels in nature, as John Muir described in the passage above. I can relate to this passage. One day when the tide was very low, a rocky strip of the shore that was usually hidden from view was exposed, and the sun, low in the west near sunset, struck those rocks and revealed a rainbow kaleidoscope of color. It was as though some cosmic jeweler had scattered thousands of tiny precious gems onto the beach. The brilliant red, green, yellow, orange, and white stones glistened among the more prevalent black and gray stones. The rocks truly did seem to "thrill with life" that day, and I felt totally alive and filled with gratitude for the pleasure of witnessing the beauty of the rocks. More than that, I felt filled with spirit and connection to the outer world.

For years, I have struggled with the concepts of faith and spirit, and to find some theology that I could relate to. I know now that nature itself, and the beach in particular, is my place of worship, and that sensory experience is my daily practice or devotional. I carry a well-worn beach rock in my pocket and rub it between my fingers in times of stress or contemplation, much like Catholics finger their rosary beads. The smoothness of the stone grounds me and brings me back to the beach. These sensory experiences are powerful evidence of being fully alive. We could regain so much of our essential natures just by paying attention to our sensory experiences instead of focusing so much on our thoughts.

Henry Beston (*The Outermost House*) lamented that our English tradition and language so often neglects the ancient and primitive sense of smell, even though smell is among the most powerful doors to deep memories and emotions. He described the various fragrances of his stretch of beach along Cape Cod in this way:

> *"So well do I know them, indeed, that were I blindfolded and led about the summer beach, I think I could tell on what part of it I was at any moment standing. At the ocean's very edge the air is almost always cool—cold even—and delicately moist with surf spray and the endless dissolution of the innumerable bubbles of the foam slides; the wet sand slop beneath exhales a cool savour of mingling beach and sea, and the innermost breakers push ahead of them puffs of this fragrant air…[On the upper beach] lies a hot and pleasant odour of sand…[I] take up a handful of the dry, bright sand, sift it slowly through my fingers, and note how the heat brings out the fine, sharp, stony smell of it." (p. 188-190)*

What a lesson for us to learn about opening the senses and really experiencing the world around us. So much of life experience passes us by because we get caught up in thoughts about the past or future, and do not engage our senses in the present moment. The beach is a sensory carnival, waiting for us to pay attention and dance with joy in its fragrant and musical wake.

Paying Attention to Emotional Responses

"On a winter afternoon near twilight, waves are coursing in from the northeast, rearing up and pouring down with a wild, pitching crash. They are plunging breakers, the kind of wave whose crest moves faster than its body, creating a smooth, glassy hollow, a tunnel in the water. The spilling breaker—a wave that breaks slowly, its crest sliding down its forward side—is rare here, and surging waves, those that move up the beach without breaking, are unheard of. Such tidy taxonomical categories give the impression of uniformity, but each

wave is unique, born of intricate combinations of breezes, planetary gyres, and tiny puffs gathered over the sea." (Jennifer Ackerman, Notes from the Shore, p. 21)

Hours of sitting on a beach watching waves transition from a swell to cresting and spilling over have convinced me that emotions have phases closely resembling waves. Anger is a perfect example. It often starts as a minor annoyance. Some thought or event, like a light wind over the ocean, tickles the surface and raises a tiny wave. We might not immediately recognize the annoyance if we are preoccupied with other things. But the feeling registers in the body, if not in conscious awareness. The wave may collapse if the wind dies down—if we recognize the thought or event as annoyance or frustration and take some action immediately to dispel it. But sometimes the wind keeps blowing and the irritation rises into a bigger swell, rolling along until it becomes full blown anger. When the wave of anger approaches the shore, the conscious part of our brain, the emotion spills over with some force much like the plunging breaker. We now recognize it as anger. It's hard to ignore at this point.

The spray from the crashing wave splashes up in the air, as we sputter, spit, foam at the mouth, and react. We think that somebody did something to me, and I did not like it. The foamy mixture of air and water, the swash, flows up the beach, filling us full of emotion and sometimes engulfing others around us, but that initial blast of feeling quickly recedes like the backwash that flows back into the sea. If it collides with another oncoming wave of emotion, it churns up a lot of sand and foam in a chaotic noisy mix that hisses and gurgles as it withdraws. If the wind is stiff, the swash hardens, like meringue, into sea foam that piles up and blows across the beach, taking much longer to dissolve back into its separate components of water and air. This stiff sea foam represents the resentment that might persist long after the initial wave of anger breaks. But eventually all the emotions pass and return to the sea.

Emotions, like waves, are transient, repeating events; they can be large and crash with great destruction, or gently flow up and down the beach. They sometimes come in quick succession, like three or four extra large waves in a row, followed by a period of calm, or they come intermittently and unpredictably. They generally start from something relatively small and only grow if we give the feeling energy. Like an ocean wave, the emotion is just energy passing over our surface. It's not our essence or nature. Like the water molecules that are put into motion by the energy of the wind, our true nature gets stirred up a bit, but does not get swept away by the energy of the emotion. Instead, water molecules and our essential natures both have the capacity to roll back into place after the energy moves on.

Sometimes, though, we get caught up in the current and stay within the emotional state for a long period of time, often doing great damage to our essential natures. These extended periods of stress can harm our bodies and spirits. The trick is to recognize that emotions are recurring transient events, like waves, and not let them define us or drive our behavior in the moment of passion. If we get caught up in the emotion and attach to the feeling or the situation, we can turn the gentle wave into a tsunami that wreaks widespread destruction when it finally lands on foreign shores.

Like the waves that we try to categorize as plunging, spilling or surging breaker, or a large or small wave, ultimately each emotion is unique and stems from multiple, changing influences, defying any neat classification. What I label as anger in one situation is a righteous indignation; in another situation, it is tinged with fear; and another time, it borders on rage. The common denominator of the emotion and the wave, is that they will pass, and they will be followed by another one. What I strive for is more time of peace between the crashing of the emotion waves. I must learn to ride out the wave like a surfer and stay ahead of the bone-crunching spillover.

Nature and Spirituality

"Is nature spirit-filled? Are the contemplation of nature and the immersion in nature forms of spiritual practice?" (Sara Warber and Katherine Irvine, Nature and Spirit, p. 135)

To many beach bums, the answer is a resounding YES. We feel the mystery and the spirit most acutely at the beach, because its wildness clearly demarcates the presence of nature. Partly this is because of the cultural split we have created between the inside and the outside worlds. Nature, in reality, is in us, and all around us, but we experience ourselves as being inside or outside. We have socially constructed ideas that the inside is "not nature" and the outside is nature. If we can bridge that gap, and bring the inside and outside back together, we could feel our own natures more easily. Until then, we need the immediacy of time spent outdoors, preferably in the wild, although our manicured gardens or yards can also be healing. Gardens can bridge the inside and outside in a safe and comfortable way, without the dangers and inconveniences of the wild. We can also bring reminders of nature into our living and workspaces in the forms of plants, shells, rocks, and photographs of our favorite places.

We go to the wild to see deer, hawks, elk, and golden eagles, yet I can look out my window in the city and see a multitude of beautiful birds, raccoons, skunks, coyote, and the wildest animals of all—human beings, engaged in all sorts of exotic behaviors. It's all a matter of perspective. The sparrow is every bit as wild as the turkey vulture, and appreciating the hovering and swooping of the hummingbird is as spiritual as a prayer. As Joanna Macy noted in *World as Lover, World as Self*, *"the world itself has a role to play in our spiritual liberation. It's very pressures, pains, and risks can wake us up—release us from the bonds of ego and guide us home to our vast, true nature"* (p.23).

That day at the beach with the glistening rocks, I did not need stained glass windows—I had the beauty of the golden ball of sun reflecting on multi-colored stones. I did not need a sermon—I had the roar of the ocean to prompt a contemplative mood where I could think the deep thoughts that came from within myself. I did not need the company of other people, because I was in communion with the birds, seals, and myriad life of the sea. Breathing the salty air charged my system with spirit, the Latin word for breath.

I still do not have a definition of spirituality that satisfies my academic brain, although I know in my heart and my gut what it is and experience it regularly. Sometimes when I am walking alone on a remote beach, I have a sensation of being filled up with love or joy and tears flow suddenly down my cheeks. Some cultures equate spirit with the physical world, as in nature worship, whereas others, including most western religions, see spirit as transcending the physical world. Here is another dualistic split between physical and transcendent that leads some to deny the importance of the physical world, a first step toward domination and destruction. My experience of love at the beach is a very physical sensation as well as a spiritual experience.

Some people, like contemporary philosopher Ken Wilber (*Integral Spirituality*) describe spirituality as a set of feelings or internal attributes such as loving kindness, compassion, love, joy, or an open heart. Some describe it as connection to others, the larger earth, or a higher power—feeling a part of some larger cosmos. The writing about spirituality that comes closest to what I feel personally has come from the authors of nature writing or ecology. For example, Tom Hayden described a philosophy of an "earth-based spirituality" in *The Lost Gospel of the Earth*. As he explained this form of spirituality, the earth is viewed as *"the birthplace, the subject and object, and burial grounds for the elements of consciousness…a living interconnected form"* (p. 2). He described how the sacred ground and seas that indigenous peoples and ancient cultures worshipped were supplanted in many formal religions by a belief that the sacred was somewhere above the earth, in the heavens, not of the earth. Hayden proposed that we need to be "born-again" in nature; an apt description of my own experience on the beach, when I was "baptized" by a sneaker wave and born into a new everyday life, and a new spiritual paradigm. Of course, most of us are not interested in returning to primitive times and conditions when people worshipped the earth and made human sacrifices to appease the terrifying sea gods. Instead, we need contemporary forms of worship that blend nature and culture, a theology that uses technology in a conscious and measured way, and that keeps us in some centered space between spirituality and material things, between solitude and meaningful social connection, and between our individual selves and the larger Nature of which we are part.

Going Deeper

1. Consider the poem from Rumi that begins this chapter. The beach is a doorsill of sorts, another of those places where the two worlds, land and sea, touch. The beach offers a doorway to awakening. Rumi advises us to "ask for what you really want." In your awakened state, what do you want? What would your ideal life look like?
1. What tempts you or lulls you into going back to sleep? Who are the people or what are the situations that push you into automatic pilot?
2. Where do you feel the most alive and awake? What circumstances facilitate that awakening?
3. How do you define spirituality? What role does nature play in your own spiritual growth? What places in nature are sacred to you?
4. Have you had an experience of transcendence or connection with the outer world? What was that like? How did it change you?

4
Essence: Being Worth Your Salt

"Fish, amphibian, and reptile, warm-blooded bird and mammal—each of us carries in our veins a salty stream in which the elements sodium, potassium, and calcium are combined in almost the same proportions as in sea water…and as life itself began in the sea, so each of us begins his individual life in a miniature ocean within his mother's womb, and in the stages of his embryonic development, repeats the steps by which his race evolved from gill-breathing inhabitants of a water world to creatures able to live on land." (Rachel Carson, The Sea around Us, p. 13-14)

How revealing is that? Our very essence, the composition of our lifeblood, is the same as the sea. A saying that was common in my youth was to describe someone whose behavior was questionable as "not worth his salt." Historically, salt was a valuable commodity, the object of much trade around the world. Being untrue to one's salty sea nature is to pretend, to be an imposter, a fraud, to be worthless. So how do we become worth our salt? This section explores the idea of essence.

What is the difference between essence and nature? According to the dictionary, essence comes from the Latin word meaning, to be. It does not mean "to think," "to play a role," or "to do." Essence is who we are at the deepest level of being, when stripped of our roles and identities. Many people equate essence with the soul—the part that makes each of us a unique person. The word nature comes from the Latin, natura, meaning birth or character, and over the years has developed many distinct meanings. Nature is the character of our world in its entirety and in juxtaposition to "human-made." We seek to "get back to nature" or take nature tours, making nature something outside of ourselves, the outdoors versus the indoors of our daily existence. Ironically, humans are "nature-made." Nature is also portrayed as a personified deity, as in Mother Nature. That image always reminds me of the old margarine commercial—"it's not nice to fool Mother Nature!" I recognize that image as a way that modern society has trivialized nature to make it easier to exploit the land and sea (and women as well).

In Christian theology, nature is located between heaven and hell, a transitional place where we exist briefly and are scrutinized for our merit. It is not home, but is a testing ground to determine whether our permanent location should be in heaven or hell. How often are images of a glorious heaven or afterworld presented to us in a way that makes our present world seem inadequate? This concept of the earth as a mere holding tank is not dissimilar to religious beliefs about re-incarnation that put us on the earth repeatedly until we have learned enough to become "enlightened" and step off the earthly cycle. These views may lead to thinking that we are temporary renters, not homeowners on the earth, thus increasing the chances that we may trash our world because we have a better one waiting for us elsewhere.

The Merriam-Webster dictionary also defines nature as *"the inherent character or basic constitution of a thing or person; humankind's original condition."* The search for discovering that original condition or inherent nature of humankind has been the source of thousands of years of wisdom writing and oral tradition throughout the world. To me, this demonstrates that people across all cultures and all time periods have faced circumstances that led them to lose themselves and obscure their true natures. Ancient wisdom teachers and contemporary psychologists both study the ways that human beings mask, hide, or lose their essence or natural characters. Identities, egos, deceptions, and false self-systems take us out of our natural condition. Cultural mechanisms of alienation, consumerism, egocentrism and ethnocentrism, nationalism, and materialism are fostered by the lack of connection to the outer world of nature. But culture is not the enemy. It only becomes a negative influence when culture becomes too estranged from the natural world. We create culture, so we can course correct to restore a balance between culture and nature. We have the power to create a "culture of nature."

Losing Our True Natures

"for whatever we lose (like a you or a me),
it's always ourselves we find in the sea."
(ee cummings, Maggie and Milly and molly and may)

Angeles Arrien, in *The Four-Fold Way,* observed that we feed our false selves through editing, rehearsing, lying, or withholding our truth. When we show a false self to the world, we abandon our true selves and lose our integrity. She noted that we abandon our true natures for five basic reasons:

1. for someone's love;
2. for someone's acceptance or approval;
3. to keep the peace;
4. to maintain balance; and
5. to stay in harmony.

For example, sometimes we avoid conflict with others to keep the peace in the short term, but in reality, we create a false sense of peace, balance, or harmony and do not really win the approval or love of the other person if they recognize that we are just appeasing them. That person learns that we can be manipulated and loses respect for us. We both end up losing. We become weak-hearted and eventually lose our own sense of self, our integrity, and feel that we don't even know ourselves anymore. We end up with the opposite of our intentions—instead of keeping the peace, we feel restless and resentful, and instead of balance, we feel off-kilter. If I have to ask, *Who am I?* I surely need to begin to reclaim my own essence. I won't find it from others, because it is already inside of me—the good and the bad parts of my essence. As much as I want to only reveal the good stuff, the bad is there as well. Our efforts to hide our flaws are generally unsuccessful, so we may as well shed our masks and be ourselves. As Oscar Wilde once declared: *"You may as well be yourself, everyone else is taken."*

The beachwise life holds promise for reclaiming the lost self. The relentless waves wash away all identities, surfaces, and pretenses; blunts the sharp edges of self-criticism and judgmental thinking into comfortable rounded corners; and leaves the deepest essence of our authentic selves. It is difficult to hang on to self-importance when faced with the enormity and power of the sea.

Life's experiences leave their mark on us. We have to contend with family expectations, social conditioning, the demands of our bosses and significant others, and pressures to fit in with a social group or with dominant culture. These can strip us of our authentic selves if we give in too often. So how do we re-discover our own nature? We can start by looking back over our lives. Angeles Arrien (*Second Half of Life*) suggested that integrating our experience and becoming our true selves, requires us to blend the five faces of our lives into one whole. These five faces are:

❖ the child, full of wonder, awe, and curiosity;
❖ the youth, brimming with creative fire and a sense of adventure;
❖ the adult, marked by experience, trustworthiness, and responsibility;
❖ the elder, which is lined with strength balanced with softness and a subtlety that reveals wisdom; and
❖ our true unique nature, with our own gifts and talents to share with the world.

This blending of our earlier experiences and unique qualities retains the positive aspects of all of our developmental stages, but leaves behind denial, indulgence, lying, distorting, judging, manipulating, comparing, competing, seducing, and cynicism. Rachel Carson would agree with this idea of re-integrating the face of the child into our adult lives. In her children's book (*Help Your Child to Wonder*), she noted

> *"A child's world is fresh and new and beautiful, full of wonder and excitement. It is our misfortune that for most of us that clear-eyed vision, that true instinct for what is beautiful and awe-inspiring, is dimmed and even lost before we reach adulthood" (p. 42).*

I have learned a lot about my own nature from observing rocks and sand, and found others who were equally enchanted by these beach elements. Gary Greenberg studies sand from around the world (*A Grain of Sand*) and what he found revealed the natural evolution of rocks from earth to sea, and back to earth again. Craggy mountain peaks are eroded by rain and shed boulders that roll into rivers. The boulders are reduced to cobbles and pebbles by the strong currents, and are washed out to sea again and again to undergo further grinding to sand. The grains of sand made from quartz, the most durable of all materials, are nearly indestructible, but the coral and other materials like shells and bony structures of sea life are eroded to clay and dust, which then compacts into soil and eventually into rocks again. I like to think of ego as undergoing this transformation—we get inflated heads the size of boulders in our younger years, but the continual battering of the waves and the intermittent gale force wind storms of our lives reduce us down to size, to those indestructible grains of quartz sand. Our essence also evolves—we are not the same people today as we were yesterday. Our journey through life smoothes out the rough edges and leaves us near the end with only our essential translucent core, those indestructible grains of quartz. In 2012, as I watched my mother succumb to cancer, she became translucent. I believe that her true essence was shining through her physical body that was ravaged by pain and anxiety. Impending death brings the essence closer to the surface and more visible.

The ocean reminds us constantly of our true nature because the water in our own physical bodies mimics the oceans, the rhythmic beating of our hearts pumps blood in waves through-out our bodies and our bodies are affected by the pull of the sun and the moon as are the ocean tides. Blood pressure measures the internal tides of our body water. Women's menstrual cycles flow with the lunar cycle, like the tides. Listening to the external rhythms of the ocean and noticing the subtle variations of the sands can open us to pay attention to our internal rhythms. We can begin to ask ourselves the hard questions and let the answers that are buried deep in our own knowing emerge.

I have learned that my essence or true nature is not the same as the identities I have constructed or adopted from society. Who am I when I let go of my identities? On the beach, I am not my profession, my role in my family, the mask I present to strangers, the controlled persona my students and coworkers see. I am not an aging, imperfect body. I am not the constant, but fleeting emotions that I experience—fear, pride, sadness, grief, joy, guilt, anxiety, anger, confusion, contentment, frustration, amusement, or moral indignation. I am not the aches and pains of my joints or the fatigue of my muscles. I am not my body or my mind, yet I am both of these and much more. I am not my memories; the happy childhood events, the losses, the good and bad of past relationships, the vacations, graduations and disappointments. I carry these memories and they affect me, but they do not define me as a person. When I shed identities, transient emotions, and memories, what is left?

I don't fully know the answer to this question about my own essential nature, but I do know I come closest to comprehending it when I am alone on a beach. In silence and solitude on a sandy beach, I come closest to being myself. When there is no other person present for comparison, no one to impress or whose needs to consider, when the cliff face demarcates a narrow strip of beach and I am between the sea and the rocks, a space opens up for contemplation. Is it the emptiness, the vastness of ocean and sky that creates this perception of an inner space? Or is it the fullness of the living ocean; not an emptiness at all? Is it the dampening of thought that comes with focusing on the rise and fall of waves? I do not know the answer yet, but I know it happens and that if I continue to stay awake, all I need to know will be revealed. Maybe I already know all I need to know, or maybe some of it is unknowable. The important thing is to stay open and awake and see what happens.

John Muir reflected on what happens when we wake up to nature. In this account, he noted the effects of spending time in the wilderness, particularly, the sight of the sun's rays penetrating through a forest canopy:

"You bathe in those spirit-beams, turning round and round, as if warming at a campfire. Presently, you lose consciousness of your own separate existence, you blend with the landscape, and become part and parcel of nature." (In Chris Highland, Editor, Meditations of John Muir, Nature's Temple, p. 121)

Perhaps that essence beyond the identities and emotions is a one-ness with nature. To find our own nature at the beach, we must preserve and protect Nature to keep those spirit beams pure. Our essence cannot be found in empty plastic bottles, Styrofoam, candy wrappers, beer cans, and other remnants of human waste tossed into the ocean to wash up on our beaches. Our nature is not to be found in the chemicals we flush through our water systems that kill the fish and pollute the waters we ultimately drink. As we learn our own true nature and nurture ourselves, we must also nurture and heal our outer homes in the sea and on the earth.

For the past several years, I have been photographing rocks. It started one day when I came home with yet another pocketful of beach stones and surveyed the hundreds of rocks already strewn around my small apartment. I decided to try leaving the rocks in their natural homes instead of trying to "domesticate" them. This photographing of rocks led to a closer examination of the stones. I started to focus on exposed rock faces in the cliffs and the massive boulders that sit upon the beach, and I began to see my life as a laying down of layers over time. Some rock faces show very clearly delineated layers, some only inches deep and others several feet in depth. Some had sharp borders between the layers, whereas others were more transitional borders merging together into overlapping and indistinct edges. Looking at those layered rock faces, I started to wonder if cut in cross-section psychically, my past would be revealed in those distinct layers. Perhaps there would be a rosy quartz layer for childhood, under a darker flinty layer for adolescence, when I began to hide my true self, layers of bright color for college when I gained rapidly in knowledge about the broader world and about ideas. There might be variegated layers, some thin and some thick that represented relationships of different intensities and lengths, and jagged cuts and scars in the rock, representing losses and emotional pain.

But most rock faces are not so distinctly layered. Many stones are multicolored, have jagged edges of different hues or textures, or have lines of stone of different colors or textures shot through them. Perhaps this represents the integrated life. The rosy quartz of childhood intermingles with adult experiences. Certain repeating or consistent features of life are represented by the lines that course through the rock in meandering patterns like a river. Perhaps there is a golden-hued line of compassion here, a sharp jagged edge that represents a traumatic event that I have not yet fully resolved, and flakes of silver or gold that represent memories of past relationships.

Rock faces often have cracks and crevasses, and I have noticed how much beach material gets lodged in these cracks—stones, seaweed, and bits of snail shells. Other sea creatures set up housekeeping in the cracks—like the barnacles, limpets, and mussels. The detritus stuck in the cracks may be the recent events that I have not yet integrated. They stick there, irritating me, until I take time to reflect on them and integrate them into the whole if they are worth keeping, or expel them as toxic influences if they are poisoning my psyche. Some are precious gems; life lessons waiting to be integrated into my authentic being.

Like trying to identify the type of stone of the rock face, it is hard to distinguish my essence from the layers of ego, identities, memories, and life experiences I have had. I could spend the rest of my life in a geological survey of my own psyche, and in fact, I have been engaged in a lot of excavation in recent years. However, the point is not to change the rock face. It is layered or integrated, smooth or rough, solid or multi-colored. It is what it is, created over millennium. Rock is the foundation of the earth. My personal foundation, my personal bedrock, reveals a lot about my character and is to be cherished, cracks, flaws, and detritus.

Simplicity

"We think of rock as a symbol of durability, yet even the hardest rock shatters and wears away when attacked by rain, frost, or surf. But a grain of sand is almost indestructible. It is the ultimate product of the work of the waves—the minute hard core of mineral that remains after years of grinding and polishing. The tiny grains of wet sand lie with little space between them, each holding a film of water about itself by capillary attraction. Because of this cushioning liquid film, there is little further wearing by attrition. Even the blows of heavy surf cannot cause one sand grain to rub against another." (Rachel Carson, The Edge of the Sea, p. 120)

  If we simplify our egos down to our essential core, those elements of our being are like the indestructible grains of sand, cushioned by the love that surrounds us. We are buffeted by the waves of daily events, but our essence is not washed away or broken. Reducing to our essential core or "going back to nature" means to shed the subterfuge, the games, manipulations, and schemes that complicate our lives. Living the truth is so much simpler. When we simplify our lives, we prioritize the activities that nurture our spirits and resist the powerful forces of distraction and consumerism in our culture. Run-off from industry poisons the earth and seas, and the toxic messages of much of our media and interpersonal conflicts poison our souls. Simplifying our lives means asking, What do I need to be happy? If we listen to the external voices, the answer might be a big screen TV, a nicer house, a fancier car, or an iPad. If we listen to our inner voices, the answer might be deeper and more satisfying relationships, love, good health, and more time to go to the beach. Usually the simpler things are better for us, and for the environment.

  Anne Morrow Lindbergh proposed that there are techniques that lead to greater harmony in our lives, and simplification is a key strategy. She noted, *"I mean to live a simple life, to choose a simple shell I can carry easily like a hermit crab"* (p. 25). Her search for simplicity was challenged by the complexities of modern living, which is a life of "multiplicity." She asked the difficult questions about how we can remain whole among all the distractions of life, how we can stay in balance when multiple forces pull us in different directions. Obviously, there are no easy answers, but *"only clues, shells from the sea"* to guide our passage.

  If we think about beach vacations, we might find some revelations. We simplify our wardrobe to what can fit into a suitcase, we strip away the excess material things, and focus on getting our entertainment from the beach. We leave behind stress and let ourselves enjoy the moment. We take off the watch and let our bodies dictate when to eat or rest. When we simplify the outsides of our existence, we can begin to simplify the inner world as well. Can we live our lives as if on a beach vacation every day? Can we scale back to the bare essentials and live each moment like we are on vacation?

Going Deeper
1. Describe yourself as you would if you were meeting someone for lunch; someone who was a potential new friend or a first date. Now think about how much of your self-description can be encapsulated as identities: your occupation, age, gender,

family background, sexual identity, race or ethnicity, marital or relationship status, religion, national origin, place of birth, and so on. Surely these are parts of your life experience, but are they who you really are? Try again with a self-description that goes beyond those identities to capturing what kind of person you are.
2. Where do you feel the most true to yourself? In what situations, or with what people, can you be yourself? Could those situations be re-created in other aspects of your life? Visualize what your life would look like if you could be yourself all the time.
3. Where do you feel the greatest need to hide, edit, or mask your true self? What situations or people create this disconnect for you? Are there ways that you can minimize your time in those situations or with those people? What would happen if you were yourself even with those people who trigger you to edit or hide yourself?

5
Flexibility, Fluidity, and other "F" Words

"The sand on a beach appears stationary to the casual observer, but beaches are actually dynamic land forms in constant change. Waves, currents, and winds drive a continual process of creation and erosion…When you stand on a beach in the water, you feel the frantic race of sand rushing past your feet. The movement of sand is so powerful that it literally undermines your footing on the shoreline."
(Gary Greenberg, A Grain of Sand, p. 54)

Look closely at the plants and trees that grow close to the ocean. They must be flexible to survive the winds, the sandy soil, and waves. The cypress trees bend over so that they do not get their upper branches snapped off by buffeting winds. Think of the myriad creatures of the sea—they must adapt to the continually changing landscape as the tides goes in and out, to harsh winds and moving sand, to violent storms and hungry predators from sea and land and sky. But the water itself is the ultimate teacher of flexibility. Water is able to flow over and around any barrier. We use fluidity, the concept of water, in our language about being adaptable, healthy, and emotionally flexible. When our fluids are not flowing easily throughout our bodies, we get sick. When blood flow is impeded by blockages in our arteries we get heart attacks and stroke. Fluid blockages in the kidneys or bile ducts cause excruciating pain. When our words cannot flow freely in a relationship, the relationship suffers. When we "dam up" our feelings, we feel stifled, but when we can be "natural," we "go with the flow" and experience "streams of consciousness." We describe someone who moves gracefully as having "fluid movements," comparing them to water.

In many cultures, loss of fluidity or emotional flexibility is associated with a concept called "soul loss," and the symptoms include apathy, confusion, doubt, depression, restlessness, loss of energy or motivation, and irritation (Angeles Arrien, *Second Half of Life*). These symptoms certainly described my "midlife crisis" which I am beginning to reframe as soul loss. It started with a loss of flexibility. This section explores two "F" words: flexibility and forgiveness. A third "F" word, fluidity, is the key to re-gaining our souls and letting our inner fluids flow freely again.

Flexibility and Human Relationships

"The beach is not so much a distinct place as it is a set of relations among four elements: earth, water, wind, and sun. Partnered in an endless dance, these elements produce a staggering range of beaches, each subject to constant change, sometimes rhythmical and cyclical, sometimes linear and catastrophic…minute by minute, hour by hour, each of the four constituents submits to the action of the others, and each in turn, bends the others to its influence." (Lencek and Bosker, The Beach: A History of Paradise on Earth, pp. 4-5)

Human relationships are much like this dance of the four elements that shape and reshape the beach. Each relationship is a different blend of the elements, and each relationship is dynamic and changes minute-by-minute. Cultivating flexibility is essential to our survival, but our minds try to convince us that stability, permanence, and constancy are the keys to a good relationship.

"Can't you be more flexible?" they asked. To me, the real meaning of this question usually was "won't you do it my way?" I was always good at compromise or finding a mutually acceptable solution to problems at work, but in my intimate relationships, I almost always gave in to keep the peace and avoid conflict, something that I inaccurately labeled as "being flexible" at the time. So "flexible" became an "F" word for me, triggering a feeling of defensiveness. The experience of letting go of a job I held for more than 20 years and opening up to new experiences taught me a big lesson about flexibility, one that I think has generalized to my personal relationships as well. Human relationships, like the beach, are a "set of relations" among many diverse elements, and one must be flexible to accommodate all the influences, but not so flexible as to break, or to lose integrity. I learned that what I was labeling as "flexible" in those early relationships was actually conflict avoidance. If I truly cultivate flexibility, I will no longer be conflict avoidant, because I will see conflict as Angeles Arrien defines it, *"an opportunity for creative problem-solving."* In some of those earlier situations, I was compromising my own integrity when I gave in to another's demands in the name of flexibility. In other instances, I was too rigid and unyielding and this inflexibility caused pain for me and for others in my life. Flexibility is on a continuum like the other qualities we have discussed. One needs to learn to be flexible enough to go with changing circumstances, but not so flexible as to be a pushover.

The beach is the best teacher of flow and fluidity. In my reading about the sea, I learned that a wave is not always water traveling over long distances. In the case of currents, water does travel, but more often, a wave is energy born mostly of wind that rolls over the ocean. The energy causes the water to rise and fall, the water molecules spinning in a circle, ending up back where they started as the energy moves on. The ocean looks like a whole; we cannot discern the separate water molecules because they all blend together to make an enormous body of water. Likewise, when we are dealing with a person who is important to us, we see the outward signs, but not the inner processes and invisible external circumstances that affect our present interaction.

I have begun to think of negative emotions or feeling upset, with this wave analogy. I think that the upset is the energy of the wind, or the situation or the person with whom I am upset, a person I can think of as a "windbag" for that brief moment. I can recognize that it will soon roll over me, and I will settle back into a state of harmony. The upset will not sweep me away if I stay connected to my own inner fluidity and let the swell of energy roll over me. It just ruffles the surface temporarily. Positive emotions are also transient events. I have learned that it is futile to desire only the positive feelings and avoid the negative. They both roll in and out of my life, like waves.

Being fluid and flexible does not mean being weak. In fact, water is a good example of the strength of fluidity. The Tao Te Ching notes: *"Under heaven nothing is more soft and yielding than water, Yet for attacking the solid and strong nothing is better. It has no equal."*

Water molecules in the seas respond to many influences: wind, currents, the sun and the moon, seismic events, and volcanoes. Most scientists agree that we humans might also influence the seas in positive and negative ways. There are the obvious ways that we have polluted the seas and the earth, but there are also more subtle forms of influence or reciprocity. Masuru Emoto (*The Hidden Messages of Water*) demonstrated that water responds to human language and prayer, creating beautiful crystals in response to words of kindness, love, art, and beauty, and warped, twisted forms when exposed to words of anger, violence, or harsh music. It is not much of a stretch to imagine that the water in our bodies also reacts to external forces. When we are constantly exposed to a hostile or violent culture, the water molecules in our body may twist in agony.

How can I keep my own salty body fluid flowing with ease, overcoming challenges and obstacles, spinning in my body in radiant crystals? I am learning to respond to requests for flexibility with greater detachment. What does the other person want? What expectations do I have? What expectations does that other person have? How can we find a solution that meets both of our needs? Can I meet this request without sacrificing my own integrity? I try to keep positive influences around me to keep my fluids flowing easily—periods of silence and solitude, music that soothes the soul and books that inspire. I try to minimize my exposure to those "windbags" of negative energy such as toxic people, too much hustle and bustle, and too much seductive consumer culture. And of course, I build in plenty of time for the beach.

Angeles Arrien (*Indepth Yearlong*) taught me that loss of sense of humor shows where I lack flexibility and have become overly attached to some outcome. When I become deadly serious about something that is the warning flag of attachment. One who is firmly attached to a particular person or outcome becomes rigid and loses flexibility. Angeles urges us to stay connected to our "funny bone." Sometimes I need to write funny stories about my experiences to see how ridiculous my attachments and fears really are. When I am able to see the humor in my past missteps, I know I am on the road to healing. Visualizations are also useful—when I'm feeling resistant and getting all rigid in my thinking, I try to picture myself attempting some impossible yoga posture to remind me about staying flexible. I have also taped a poem to my refrigerator door to remind of the value of flexibility: *"I would love to live like a river flows, Carried by the surprise of its unfolding"* John O'Donohue (quoted in Angeles Arrien, *Second Half of Life*, p. 31).

Rigidity is about trying to control some event or person, but control is mostly illusory. As I started writing this section, I had a subheading in my outline titled, "turning the tide." Later, when I re-read it, I realized how ludicrous it was. I can no more turn the tide than I can change the lunar cycles or make another person love or respect me. The key to success as a human is to learn where I have real choices (mostly my own behavior and reactions) and where I have no control. As the old adage says, grant me the wisdom to know the difference!

Forgiveness

"Nearness to the sea destroys pettiness." (French saying of the late 1800s)

Now let's address the ultimate "F" word--forgiveness. Like many humans, I sometimes carry grudges for a long time. One of the greatest challenges I have faced in the past few years has been learning how to forgive both myself and other people for past harms. This is all about letting go of the past. Angeles Arrien (*Indepth Yearlong*) taught me that the past is not a place of power. It is too easy to get stuck in the stories of the past and drive those stories down a road of "wound-ology" and victimhood. This trip takes us further down the treacherous path of unhealthy ego, in the opposite direction of wisdom. Holding on to the old grievances has not yet earned me martyr status, except in my own mind, so it's time for them to go.

If instead, the past is viewed as a path of initiation, and those painful events are considered as rites of passage, important lessons about life, or tests of courage, patience, or flexibility, they are to be honored as gifts along our wisdom path. Forgiveness is a first step to putting the past into perspective and not allowing the past to control our capacity to be fully present in the moment; the now when life is actually lived.

I admit that this is easier said than done. I have one person in particular that I have found very hard to forgive. I have given way too much power to this person to make me feel resentful and puffed up with righteous indignation, even now, almost ten years after the offensive events took place. The lesson I am learning from examining this situation is that I hold on to grudges when I feel I have been treated unfairly. I want justice to be done. I want that person to see how wrong she is (in other words, how "wronged" I have been).

I have come to learn that the lesson for me in this instance is about pride. I am invested in having others see me as a person of integrity, so if that image is challenged in any way, I get defensive and ruminate about the situation for weeks, months, or in this one situation, for years. What good does this do me? I cannot control what another person thinks of me, and nothing I say is likely to change that person's opinion. All I can do is practice integrity, knowing that most people will see it. Integrity is in my actions, the alignment of words and deeds, not in my words alone.

I have to look at my pridefulness, and its close cousin, arrogance, and determine why I'm hanging on to this grievance. I cannot change the events of the past, but I can change my perceptions of those events, reflect on what I've learned from the experiences, and change my current behavior accordingly. If I can see these experiences as blessings, or as opportunities to learn something about myself, I can forgive more easily. This is theoretical, of course, since I have not yet reached the point of forgiving this particular person in my life. I'm hanging on to it for a reason, but I have yet to identify the reason. But I am beginning to see the experience as more of a blessing than a curse, and that's the first step toward forgiving. Sometimes I think that a little bit of hanging on to it keeps me more vigilant so that I do not place myself in a similar situation in the future. The challenge is to remember the lesson, but without the resentment. Maybe the saying should be "forgive but don't forget."

I used to think that righteous indignation was a good thing—it meant I was "right" didn't it? It meant that I had identified an injustice that needed to be addressed before I could forgive the person. Then a quote from Oscar Wilde stopped me in my tracks one day. Moral indignation, he said, was "jealousy with a halo." It made me consider that the person who had wronged me had something that I wanted and could not have, therefore, my out of proportion response to the event was because I was trying to hide my jealousy under the veneer of injustice. It was rather a humbling experience to have to examine how I sometimes lapsed into moral superiority to mask other motives.

Angeles Arrien (*Second Half of Life*) noted that there are three forms of forgiveness work that we must practice regularly. If we aim to gain wisdom, we need to:

1) Forgive ourselves for the harm we have done to ourselves by participating in self-deception or giving up our essential nature to please others;
2) Forgive those we have harmed, do reparation work, and commit that we will not repeat the harmful behavior; and
3) Forgive those who have hurt us, demonstrating our willingness to let go of these past resentments, disappointments, and pains.

Reparation work begins with true apology—done sincerely and genuinely, not from a motivation of appeasement or trying to please or impress others. Too often in the past I said I was sorry about something just to avoid further conflict---I did not really mean it. Resentments continued to build up and the relationship suffered from my lack of honesty.

When we recognize that we have harmed someone else because of our actions, and we do not address our responsibility, this leads to regret. Regrets can morph into shame and guilt; potentially paralyzing feelings that keep us stuck in the soup of inaction, stewing in negativity. If we experience the feeling as remorse instead of regret, we can immediately move to acts of reparation, and learn from the experience to change our future behavior, ensuring that we do not cause this type of hurt again. Taking action deflects the guilt and shame and helps us reconnect with our authentic self.

As I was writing this section, I took a short break to check my email. A friend had forwarded a message to me about forgiveness. The subject line read ***For Giving***. It made me reflect more deeply about the concept, and the need to give up grudges for the purpose of giving. By forgiving myself, I was giving away the pain and by forgiving others, I was giving healing energy to myself and other people. This email also pointed out to me the role of synchronicity. If I reflect deeply on some issue and need clarity, if I'm open to recognizing it, answers or insights will come to me. Sometimes the answer is within me, and will rise if I am still and silent, and sometimes it comes as a gift from the outside world.

Going Deeper
1. Consider how flexible you are in the different domains of life: in your work, with your family, with friends, and in your intimate relationships. Within your own nature, how flexible are you physically, emotionally, cognitively, and spiritually? If you find any signs of rigidity, what actions can you take to increase your flexibility?
2. What situations often lead you to lose your sense of humor? These are the places where we are overly attached to some outcome and are not exercising flexibility. Can you reframe the situation to see the humor in it? Try making up a silly story or create a visual image of the situation that highlights the humor in it.
3. Who do you need to forgive? Make a list of people in your life that you feel have wronged you. Now think about why you are holding on to the grudge, and what effect it might be having on your own life. How would your life change if you forgave those people?
4. Now list the people you feel you have wronged. Can you make amends? Can you forgive yourself for harming others? How can you change your own behavior so as to not engage in those harmful behaviors in the future?
5. In what ways have you harmed yourself? Are you ready to forgive yourself? How would life be different if you did not harbor grudges against yourself?

6
Patience or Slowing to a Beach Rhythm

"one should lie empty, open, choiceless as a beach—waiting for a gift from the sea."
(Anne Morrow Lindbergh, Gift from the Sea, p. 17)

One day when I arrived at the beach soon after sunrise, I saw thousands of iridescent blue objects strewn along the beach. As shown in the picture above, the by-the-wind sailor is a sort of jellyfish that I had never seen before and only rarely seen since. My introduction to them was a "gift from the sea." No matter how much I'd like to see one again, I have to be patient and wait for another gifting; perhaps I'll never see another one. The beach moves to its own rhythm with its own weather. You cannot hurry the tides, make the sun penetrate the fog, or control the wind. You cannot will the seals to appear or for a beautiful shell or starfish to materialize. You must be patient for the gift from the sea to arrive in its own time and its own way. Angeles Arrien gently reminded me that healing and personal growth cannot take place at a fast pace, but only in nature's rhythm. Spending time on the beach has the capacity to suspend time, and to free us from the frantic pace of daily life. It silences the incessant clamor of advertisements, TV, and traffic. The body can recover from the onslaught of deadlines, fueled by caffeinated beverages that encourage us to "hurry up." But hurry up for what? What has this focus on speed given to our lives? Has it improved the quality of life? On the beach, the slow, rhythmic rise and fall of waves overpowers all else and restores our natural rhythm. Why do we so cherish vacations? Is it because we slow to our natural rhythm when we are not tied to our daily routines? Is it because this slowing down of our nature cultivates patience and ultimately brings us peace? In this section, I want to contemplate how slowing down to nature's rhythm is an underlying factor in developing patience.

The beach is a great teacher of patience. Have you ever been so anxious to get to the water that you started to run, and then encountered that dry, shifting sand that makes you slip and slide and lose your balance? You have to slow down and move more cautiously until you reach the firmer ground closer to the water. In life, as at the beach, you have to have a firm foundation to move forward with confidence, and patience is the key to getting us there.

Patience

"Adopt the pace of nature: her secret is patience." (Ralph Waldo Emerson)

Patience is a big lesson of the beachwise philosophy. According to the dictionary, patience is the ability to tolerate delay, troubles, or suffering without becoming angry or upset. It comes from the Latin, patientia, to suffer. Suffering, tolerating, troubles…these don't sound like much fun. I think that a beachwise lesson of patience can be softer and gentler than those concepts. Beachwise patience means not hurrying to action when the path is not clear; it means waiting for the right moment to act, knowing that all things will come with grace and ease when the time is right.

Many events in our daily lives can spark impatience. For example, impatience is often triggered when another person has some characteristic that we have ourselves and wish to hide or not acknowledge. I had that revelation one day when a coworker was telling a lengthy story that I perceived to be very dull. I was chafing at the bit, trying to look interested, but internally plotting my escape route. Then I remembered Angeles Arrien's wise words, relating how other people can be mirrors that reflect back our own shadow sides. I realized that I fear that people perceive me as dull and uninteresting, and I projected my fear on this person who was exhibiting a behavior that I wanted to avoid. I made a conscious decision to really listen to the person, and found a point of connection that turned the story from a monologue into a conversation that was engaging for both of us.

Impatience also rears its ugly head when we are attached to particular outcomes and want those outcomes to manifest NOW! Craving or strong desire for particular events or things also contributes to impatience. When we attach firmly to some event or outcome, we lose our flexibility. Patience is closely related to flexibility, maintaining a sense of humor, and staying curious. Patience is the ability to let go of expectations, another word for attachments. Those expectations for how things are supposed to go can underlie impatience, which often leads to impetuous actions that can harm us, and the people around us.

Impatience can also be triggered when we move out of the present moment and set our sights on the past or the future. I wonder if that human capacity to anticipate, the ability to think of events that happened in the past or might happen in the future, has the downside of leading to impatience. Most animals have to be patient to survive. I watch seabirds bobbing on the waves, waiting for a fish to manifest. If the bird gets impatient and flies away too soon, they may starve. Evolution of the human brain has certainly given humans many benefits, but the by-products may be impatience, disappointment, guilt, and depression. When I look to the past, I often feel impatience over my self-perceived inability to let go of old attachments, or my reluctance to forgive. When I look to the future, I often feel impatient when I anticipate "brighter days" ahead. I look forward impatiently to the next beach walk or vacation day rather than focus on what I'm doing at the moment, especially if it is one of the activities I don't particularly like, such as laundry or cleaning the toilet.

Patience was one of my biggest lessons in the transition from Midwest farmland to west coast beach bum, and the transition from a mostly asleep-at-the-wheel mentality and automated life to one of awakening and growing. When I had the beach epiphany to "go west, middle-aged woman," I wanted it to happen right away. I chafed at the slowness of the process of packing, getting rid of belongings, and finding another job. I felt deep despair at job rejections, only to recognize later what a blessing those early rejections were. In my impatience to move, I applied for jobs that would probably have made me miserable. I eventually hobbled together three part-time temporary jobs that gave me financial breathing room for a year. I stopped applying for any job that was remotely within my expertise and I waited for the right one. Once I trusted that it would happen, the perfect job materialized. In other words, when I practiced patience, the right situation came to me easily. I think that the beach fostered that patience. When feeling job anxiety, I went to the beach and allowed the ocean breezes to blow the anxiety away as I tried a "one day at a time," "live for the moment" philosophy. Uncertainty became a familiar companion; not quite a friend, but not the evil enemy either. On retrospect, while still in Iowa and chafing to leave, I was learning about transitions, closure, and starting anew. I needed that time to close well, and begin a new life well. I learned extremely valuable lessons when I examined the roots of my impatience.

Now that things are more settled in my life, I find impatience stemming from other sources, most notably when I am focused on the future or when I feel "bored." Both of these seem to be related to a perception that I want to be somewhere else or doing something different than what I'm doing. If I'm actually present with what I'm doing, I generally don't feel bored or impatient. This change sometimes amazes me. I remembered my habitual state of impatience about ten years ago when I was recovering from a break-up. I felt lost and found myself doing anything I could to distract myself from the pain of the break-up, which if I let myself think about it, led to self-blame and self-judgment. I could barely stand my own company, so I rushed to fill my life with activities. But the moment I came home from these events, the emptiness and loneliness were still there, waiting for me. I was impatient to move past the pain of the break-up and "get on" with my life, but that incessant activity prevented me from grieving and doing what I really needed to do to move on. How often do we prolong our suffering after some loss by being impatient and distracting ourselves from grieving?

With maturation, I find I am more willing to sit alone, in silence, preferably on a beach, and experience my feelings. I am less likely to seek out others to "cure" what ails me, and I recognize that the cure is inside me. In fact, as I have felt more connected to my authentic self, I rather enjoy my own company, and often consciously choose solitude. That solitude allows me to explore my own creativity, cultivate my sense of humor, and write in new and more fulfilling ways. I started to write humor essays, exploring the more hilarious aspects of some of my behaviors. It's really quite amusing to consider the convoluted ways that we try to mask our insecurities and fears to make us look better or more adult. Sometimes when I can put this absurdity into words, I crack myself up! I now realize that amusing myself is much more important than amusing others. It is a sign of self-acceptance and self-appreciation that I lacked in my younger years. Patience is one of the keys to coming back to my own unique nature, and my own sense of humor.

Another beach experience that taught me about patience occurred one sunny day at Rodeo Lagoon. I was crossing the footbridge to the beach, when I noticed a great blue heron standing in about six inches of water at the edge of the calm lagoon. The bird was completely motionless and blended with the background. I'm not sure why I even noticed it. I stood at the rail watching the bird for about 15 minutes. It patiently maintained its stillness until an unsuspecting fish swam between its spindly legs and the sharp beak snapped up the fish in a silver flash. Patience won the prize—a tasty morsel. I realized that cultivating patience through stillness and silence has brought me many scrumptious rewards as well.

Slowing to Nature's Rhythm

"Nature's rhythm is medium to slow" (Angeles Arrien)

Most of us must engage in this struggle for patience with all the competing demands from work, traffic, deadlines, family, friends, and neighbors. How can we learn patience when there are so many demands on us? External forces, such as the entertainment and advertising media, also create cravings and desires that tax our patience. These messages often urge us to satisfy our cravings immediately. Our consumer culture creates and reinforces short attention span and the need for constant stimulation and speed. Healing cannot take place in the fast lane.

Learning patience comes from slowing down to our natural rhythms and regarding our cravings and desires with compassion. Our materialistic culture urges us to want things and to gratify our desires immediately. I once heard a story about the Dalai Lama's visit to Los Angeles several years ago. Each day, a car took him the few miles from his hotel to the place where the workshop was being held, and he viewed the profusion of billboards and neon signs of retail stores. After a few days, he noted that even though he did not know what most of the products were, he felt a craving for them. Even the highest spiritual leader in our contemporary world can be affected by media messages! This was a powerful story for me, highlighting how vigilant I must be to those messages. I have observed that many messages in the media foster impatience and result in speeding up. There are many books, TED talks, and blogs devoted to time management and success as an academic, and most of these promote working longer hours and working faster, rather than focusing on quality, which takes patience and time to reflect.

Stephanie Kaza, editor of a book called *Hooked*, noted that the U.S. started to develop a collective consumer identity in the 1920s with the onset of packaged, processed foods and advertising of brands. Certain brands were touted as status symbols, and our identities began to revolve around our material possessions, leisure time was devoted to spending money, and the belief that owning things led to happiness was cemented in our national psyche. A consumer identity is in opposition to an ecological identity, because high levels of consumption unnecessarily deplete the earth's resources and create the craving and addiction to things that harm people, animals, and the physical environment. Because our capitalist society wants us to consume more and more, faster and faster, patience is not a virtue extolled in our society, so we need to turn to nature to learn it.

The ocean and its beaches are ancient beings and demonstrate how much time is compressed in our culture, as we look for instant gratification for our own desires. Rachel Carson (*The Sea Around Us*) estimated that the oceans were formed over two billion years ago, and that sand arose from the slow erosion of the landmasses down rivers and streams to the sea via rain, glaciers, and floods. The beaches are still works in progress, eternally changing and evolving. Beaches were not created over night, but were the result of hundreds of millions of years of evolution.

I have learned that sitting on the beach and meditating on the waves will quickly restore my own rhythm so that I can distinguish my natural desires and needs from those created by the media or other external forces, such as the demands or expectations of others. On the beach, I feel those hungers and pressures melt away as I listen to my own body wisdom. If I have patience with a craving and recognize that it is a transient feeling that will last only a few seconds if I do not feed it with attention, it will soon pass.

In the Still of the Night

"When anxious, uneasy and bad thoughts come, I go to the sea, and the sea drowns them out with its great wide sounds, cleanses me with its noise and imposes a rhythm upon everything in me that is bewildered and confused."
(Rainer Maria Rilke)

Have you ever had one of those nights when your mind and/or body could not relax enough to fall asleep? I have found that after a very busy day or week or if I have a deadline looming, I have much difficulty being still. My body and mind have habituated to tension, anxiety, and frenetic movement, and I cannot relax. As long as I am in that physical and mental state of restless movement, I feel preoccupied and tense, qualities that are not conducive to the inner peace that I desire. One of my greatest pleasures is the sensory experience of walking on a deserted beach until I feel physical fatigue. Then I burrow my body partway into a sand dune and listen to the symphonic sounds of the ocean. Sometimes I can recreate that sensation at home. I visualize the experience of the warm sand enveloping me and supporting my body. I can feel the cool breezes washing over me, the cry of the seagull, and crash of the waves, and then the tension drops away and I can be still. If I feel too impatient and want that stillness NOW, I will not achieve it. Impatience is incompatible with stillness. Impatience is about the need for speed and doing; stillness is about nature's rhythm and being.

So the lesson is that patience can be cultivated by practicing stillness and having compassion for my cravings, recognizing that I have a choice whether to indulge them or not, and knowing the consequences of indulgence. If I respect the sea and the land, I will make better choices that are healthier for me and for the earth.

Going Deeper
1. What situations or people trigger impatience for you? Closely examine these situations to see what underlies the impatience.
2. Are you more patient with others than with yourself? What about your own nature triggers impatience?
3. How much are you influenced by the consumer culture? Do you find yourself wanting things that you don't need and can't afford? How can you treat these desires with compassion, but resist them all the same?
4. Is your impatience triggered more by memories of the past or thoughts of the future? How can you shift the focus to the present moment and find peace in whatever you are doing?
5. How much time in a typical week do you spend in stillness and silence? Where can you find the time in your day to practice brief moments of still silence?

7
Peace and Love, Man

"Emotions are carried out to sea. We are even free of thoughts, at least of their articulation; clean and bare as whitened driftwood; empty as shells, ready to be filled up again with the impersonal sea and sky and wind." (Anne Morrow Lindbergh, Gift from the Sea, p. 101)

When I was a child, I remember my mother often lamenting her lack of "peace and quiet." At the time, I had no idea what she was talking about. I was acclimated to the noise and chaos endemic in a house with seven children, five of them boys who like to wrestle, strew toy soldiers all over the house, and generally run underfoot. Our household was a hub for the neighborhood kids and always bustling. As an adult, I started to see the relationship between the concepts of peace and quiet. Peace is an inner quiet that can sustain me even when the outer world is full of noise and chaos. I also learned that inner peace is a precursor to compassion and love, the qualities that make life worth living. I learned how to find that peace and quiet mostly outdoors, where the waves can set emotions and thoughts adrift. Peace is not the absence of thoughts and emotions, but a feeling of self-compassion that recognizes the thoughts and emotions as transient, like so much driftwood and seaweed underfoot for the moment, but soon gone with the next high tide.

Peace

"Every time we walk along a beach some ancient urge disturbs us so that we find ourselves shedding shoes and garments or scavenging among seaweed and whitened timbers like the homesick refugees of a long war." (Loren Eiseley)

Yes, indeed, the beach seems to me to be a place of refuge from the battlefields of life. The beach restores that elusive quality we call peace. But what is peace really? We use the word to describe the lack of war, as well as the lack of interpersonal conflict, or as an internal sensation of not being at war with our own nature. Our contemporary society certainly reinforces images of war. We try to "conquer nature," we engage in a war of the sexes, a holy war (or unholy war, depending upon one's perspective), a war against poverty, and a war against drugs. In my youth, the anthem of the junior choir at my church was "Onward Christian Soldiers," a sentiment that I always found disturbing and was part of the reason that I left formal religion as soon as I left my parent's home. We battle depression and obesity, pit forces against the powers of evil in video games and movies. Where do we learn to wage peace? Is peace a lack of emotions, or an emotional state itself? I'm clear about the effects of war, but less certain about how peace works. The human language may be incapable of truly capturing the concept of peace. For example, the new testament of the Christian Bible describes "the peace that passes all understanding."

So this may be a concept that is better understood by what it is not—peace is not conflict, striving, comparing, judging, manipulating, controlling, or competing. Angeles Arrien (*Indepth Yearlong*) proposed that the self-critical, doubting, judgmental war-mongering voices within us are the root of all violence. If we can calm these internal voices and accept ourselves, we will no longer rage against ourselves and against others, creating drama, chaos, conflict, and war. The doubting mind engages in comparison with others, always a dangerous act. Either we fall short of the other and feel insufficient and threatened, or we feel superior to the other, bolstering ego and false pride. Peace stems from self-love, clarity, and from accepting others for who they are without comparison or judgment. A tall order, indeed.

When situations or people disturb our sense of peace, we feel upset, that vague uncomfortable state of emotion that signals something is wrong. Feeling upset is the emotional equivalent of the physiological stress reaction—physically we feel our pulses race, have sweaty palms, and feel an adrenal surge in our bodies that prompts us to "fight or flight." We interpret this reaction in our bodies by cognitively assessing the situation. If there is an identifiable reason for it in the external world, like a giant wave or a city bus bearing down on us, we interpret it (rightly) as fear. But in many stressful situations, such as interpersonal conflicts, we may not be able to immediately identify the threat, so the feeling stays a vague anxiety or a generalized feeling of discomfort, uncertainty or apprehension. It is difficult to take an action to dispel the feeling of upset if we cannot identify the underlying cause.

So we often we try to escape the upset, because the feelings are uncomfortable and confusing. I know for myself that I'd rather do just about anything to avoid that feeling of distress, anxiety, uncertainty, and dread. What if, instead, we stay in the moment with the feeling of upset, recognizing that it is a transient state, and wait for what underlies it to be revealed? Is the emotion that causes the upset one of anger, fear, embarrassment, sadness, or shame? Once the emotion has been named, then we can take an action to relieve it. If strong emotions are indulged for too long, they can move to drama and become all about the story. If an action is taken to resolve the situation, we can move on and peace is restored.

When that feeling of upset is prolonged over time or often repeated, we call it "stress." Peter Kahn, in *The Human Relationship with Nature,* noted that more than 100 scientific studies have found a link between spending time in nature and stress reduction. The Japanese have a concept called "forest bathing"—the idea that just walking in the woods bathes one in peace and harmony. I love a good walk in the woods, but for me, the beach is an ideal place to reflect on the situations that cause "upset" so that we are better able to identify the underlying emotion when it happens again. Some of us are slow processors and are hard put to identify the underlying emotion at the time of the event. We need to restrain ourselves from responding at the time of the incident, but instead ride with the feeling with grace, and take the issue to the beach or the woods to process. Then perhaps we can identify what has really been "disturbing the peace" and deal with it. It's hardly ever just the recent event, but instead is fraught with past behaviors that the same person has exhibited, and similar situations with other people in the past, and our own shadows and fears. These all build up over time into patterns of behavior or responding to situations that complicate our relationships.

Peace is a companion to compassion and love. If we can find the peace within ourselves, then we can extend it to others. To feel compassion means to open our hearts to give and receive love from others, and from the world around us. Compassion does not arise easily from the upset, doubting, or conflicted heart, but flows naturally from the state of peace.

Compassion

"The least movement is of importance to all nature. The entire ocean is affected by a pebble." (Blaise Pascal)

In the past year, I have been contemplating the relationships between love and compassion. Compassion comes from the Latin word meaning "to suffer with," showing its etymological link to the word patience. If we cannot "suffer with" or be patient with our own feelings, we are unlikely to be able to deal with the feelings of other people. Compassion starts at home, with treating ourselves gently, recognizing that "to err is human." Mistakes are not disasters, but opportunities to learn new lessons and change our course. I know that I tend to have more compassion for others than for myself. Every time I make a mistake (which is daily), I berate myself. I tell myself unproductive things like, "You are supposed to be an intelligent human being, how can you do such stupid things?" Or I might despair, "Will I ever learn?" When I have a momentary lapse in my self-compassion, it affects my whole wellbeing, like the pebble that affects the entire ocean. I do notice that these inner punishing tirades are not as vitriolic as they used to be, and they don't last as long before I recognize them for what they are. I can see the humor in this self-punishment and sometimes visualize myself with the whips of self-flagellation poised, and stop before the lashes tear my skin.

Even though I'm harder on myself than I am on most other people, I still find myself judging certain other people, particularly around political, moral, or ethical issues. I find it very hard to have compassion for the war-mongers of U.S. government, for the corporate heads fighting to limit the effects of conservation efforts or those who block legislation to reduce global warming, who obstruct health care reform, for the opponents of same-sex marriage or women's rights over decisions about their bodies, for those who want to build fences at the borders, for white supremacists and others who hate people for the color of their skin or their religion, and for many others, who in my mind, are spreading hate, division, and destruction. I marvel at the Buddhist teachers who treat all individuals with compassion and wonder how they do it. I have not learned yet how to extend compassion to all. In fact, it seems clear to me that resistance and fighting for human rights and ecological efforts to save the earth are necessary for our survival—how can that be done with compassion for those hell-bent on destroying the earth and it's people?

Joanna Macy (*World as Lover, World as Self*) reminds us of the Buddhist concept of "co-rising," meaning that the institutions of society depend on our collective consent, and that self and society are interdependent. So if I am unhappy with government leaders or other people who share the same "society" as I do, I am responsible. I must figure out what I can do to change the circumstances and help to co-create a society built on compassion, love, respect, and harmony. I have an obligation to teach others, and to exercise my rights to vote and to advocate for change. I have an obligation to speak the truth about social injustices and if necessary, take actions to support nonviolent, compassionate treatment of all people and all living things.

I know that shedding ego and opening up to the myriad forms of life around me at the beach is a beginning point for cultivating compassion. John Hay (*In Defense of Nature*) described a day spent on the coast when he came upon a group of boys, one of whom had just speared an ocean sunfish. The fish, badly wounded was lying on its side in the water. When the boy pulled out the spear, the fish

> *"veered off dully into the water, while blood poured out and a little flood of water was ejected from its gills. Then I saw, or thought I saw, such rolling despair and final fright in its eyes as to make me want to run away, and there was nowhere to run to, except inside myself and inescapable humanity."*
> *(p. 163)*

If we spend time in nature and look into the eyes of other living beings or carefully study the trees and rocks, it is hard not to impose our own emotions on them. Some might dismiss John Hay's comments as anthropomorphizing, because how can we know what a fish feels? We can barely understand the experiences of other humans at times. How arrogant it seems to me not to recognize pain in these nonhuman beings. Compassion must extend beyond humans to all the living things of the earth and seas. Sometimes I find it easier to practice compassion with a bird or a crab than with another human being who has a very different worldview than I have. I can see how much work I have to do in this area, because until I am filled with compassion, my capacity to love and to gain wisdom is limited. That pebble of judgment is blocking my entire maturation. I still need to learn how to separate my displeasure and disapproval about human behaviors from the human being who behaves in bad ways from time to time, but deserves my compassion.

Love

"My soul is full of longing for the secret of the sea,
And the heart of the great ocean sends a thrilling pulse through me."
(Henry Wadsworth Longfellow)

The word love comes from the Old English word meaning "to please" or "desire." We use the word to mean so many things in our lives, that I decided to examine these varieties of love, starting with the dictionary definitions. Here is what I found, in part, in Merriam-Webster's dictionary. There were more than 14 definitions of love, including:

1. strong affection for another arising out of kinship or personal ties (maternal *love* for a child);
2. attraction based on sexual desire**;** affection and tenderness felt by lovers;
3. affection based on admiration, benevolence, or common interests (*love* for his old schoolmates);
4. an assurance of love (give her my *love*);
5. warm attachment, enthusiasm, or devotion (*love* of the sea);
6. the object of attachment, devotion, or admiration (baseball was his first *love*);
7. a beloved person: **DARLING** —often used as a term of endearment;
8. *British* —used as an informal term of address ("Hello, love");
9. unselfish loyal and benevolent concern for the good of another: as the fatherly concern of God for humankind or brotherly concern for others;
10. a person's adoration of God;
11. a god or personification of love (Venus, goddess of love that you are);
12. an amorous episode: **LOVE AFFAIR**;
13. the sexual embrace: **COPULATION**;
14. a score of zero (as in tennis) — **at love:** holding one's opponent scoreless in tennis.

I had many reactions to this list of definitions. First, I was quite thrilled to see the fifth one: love of the sea. That dictionary writer must be a kindred spirit. But mostly I was confused. How does one make any sense of all these uses of the same word? I find it interesting that the dictionary has one definition for a fatherly or brotherly kind of love—which they define as unselfish, loyal, and benevolent, but a different definition of maternal love. There is no definition for "sisterly" love like there is for "brotherly" love. Why the oversight? Why is love "gendered" in this way? This language helps to perpetuate sexist stereotypes that men cannot be good parents (they cannot "mother") and that "sisterly" love is different and less than "brotherly" love.

And how on earth did the tennis use of "love" come about? To hold an opponent scoreless, to soundly defeat an opponent sounds like the adolescent "love games" I have often heard about when people compete for sexual conquests. This definition of love is so contrary to our usual understandings of the term. These dictionary definitions were more confusing than useful in my quest to understand love, so I turned next to academic writers for enlightenment.

Some researchers try to find neurochemical explanations for love reactions, but it seems to me that this "science of attraction" is seriously flawed by focusing too much on our biology, and by its almost exclusive focus on romantic love. When I go to the beach, I often feel an expanding of my heart, and a resultant feeling of benevolence and compassion that extends to all who cross my path, and even those who enter my thoughts. The coworker with whom I am annoyed seems less aggravating when I think of her at the beach. When I am in the "beach zone," I feel a love that is not attached to sexual attraction or blood kinship. This is the type of spiritual love that fosters personal growth and improves the quality of our lives, but virtually all the biological research on love focuses on sexual attraction. Love and sex so often get conflated in research, in the media, and in our real lived experiences. The biological researchers were not very helpful in understanding love, so I looked to psychology.

Experts on the psychology of love have identified different types of love. For example, Robert Sternberg (*The Triangle of Love*) described a triangle with three points: passion, commitment, and intimacy. If we have passion only, that is a "crush." If we have intimacy and commitment, but not passion, that describes our love for family and friends—love that is close and enduring but not sexual or romantic. If we have commitment and passion, but no intimacy, that pattern might indicate a romantic relationship in its early stages, or a long-term relationship where the partners have little in common or do not communicate well. This triangle definition helps somewhat by classifying different types of relationships that we can have, but is love really only defined by these three qualities? What about compassion, honesty, integrity? Sternberg tells part of the story of love, but not enough to satisfy my need for understanding about a broader, spiritual form of love.

Love also changes as we develop from youth to maturity. As children, we are supposed to love and be loved by our parents and other adults in our lives. In adolescence, we begin to explore romantic and sexual love, and extend our love outside the family more than we did in childhood. We develop "best friends" whom we love and trust. As young adults, we experiment with close romantic relationships, trying to combine passion and intimacy into significant other relationships, and many of us have children and learn about parental love. We learn how to balance relationships—friendships with significant others and family. Many experts suggest that in midlife we begin to reconsider love, and that generativity, a drive to give back our blessings, gifts, and talents to others, opens us to a more mature type of love. Finally, in our elder years, we become more capable of transcendent love, recognizing the infinite capacity of love that extends well beyond our physical bodies. If we cannot transcend our bodies, we get stuck in an egoic, self-centered focus on our physicality that interferes with growth and evolution of spirit.

One big hurdle to experiencing love is that almost all the popular writing as well as psychological research and theory glamorize the idea of love as attachment to a certain person or people. Oh, how much pain those attachments cause us in real life. Is it possible to feel a truly detached love for all, one that is free of attachment—that "brotherly" love for the wellbeing of all? On the beach, one can feel the type of love that comes to all who gather at the shore—nature does not cast out the gossips, polluters, the exploiters, or the murderers. The sun shines on us all equally and the fog engulfs us regardless of our character. I see that I have many lessons yet to learn about love. After years of the media-influenced adrenaline-charged attractions that soon burned out, I yearned to experience a significant other relationship that was freer of attachment and angst than my previous relationships. As I thought about future intimate relationships, a snip of a song pops into my head, "I want a lover who won't make me crazy." I know that some level of attachment is inevitable—I have to feel some kind of bond or the relationship would not be a "significant other" type. Without attachment, any other would do. In my heart, I know that a relationship can be forged on grounds that are mutual, not clingy or unequal. As I grow in self-compassion and self-love, that kind of relationship seems more possible. Maybe someday songs will be written about sane, mature love rather than the typical songs today that describe love as wild, passionate, and out of control.

I've been focusing on love for another person, but really, the heart of the matter is self-love. If I cannot experience love and appreciation for myself, I am not going to be able to fully love another. Love and compassion start at home, in one's own heart. Where's the dictionary definition that focuses on self-acceptance, self-trust, self-compassion, and the other components of self-love? It seems like we are missing a great opportunity to learn about love if we only focus our attention outside, to other people and beings and the earth. We live within our own skin 24/7 with constant opportunities to practice love and compassion with ourselves. I used to be a list-maker when it comes to intimate relationships. Every time I experienced a break-up, I would create a new list of characteristics that I wanted, or didn't want, in a lover. I usually had two sections: non-negotiables and things that I would like, but did not absolutely need. Never in those years did it ever occur to me to apply that list to myself. Did I meet my own criterion as a lover of myself? Once I become the respectful, funny, loyal, affectionate, kind lover to myself, then I'll be more capable of extending those qualities to another person.

Going Deeper
1) What does it mean to you to be "at peace?" What situations foster a feeling of peacefulness for you?
2) Think of all the people that you currently "love." What role does compassion play in those relationships?
3) Do you love yourself? Do you have compassion when you make mis-steps? What aspects of yourself do you need to view with more compassion?
4) How do you define love? What qualities do you think make for a good intimate partner relationship? A good friendship?
5) Do you love yourself? In what areas do you fall short as a lover to yourself?

8
Reflection and Integration

"The voice of the sea speaks to the soul. The touch of the sea is sensuous, enfolding the body in its soft, close embrace." (Kate Chopin, The Awakening)

Wisdom arises when we engage in a process of reflecting on life experience to see the patterns and then integrating that knowledge into our being so that we can avoid making the same mistakes in future actions. Wisdom allows us to resolve past traumas by letting them go and forgiving. Integration of life's lessons is a complex business, and we often find ourselves appalled when we seem not to learn from our previous mistakes. One day I had a profound insight and furiously wrote the idea in my journal. I was so proud of myself for making this connection. A little later, I was flipping back through my journal, and found much to my dismay, that two weeks earlier, I had written about the same insight in almost identical words. WTF???? How could this be? Obviously I had not integrated this insight into my life; I had let the thought be a fleeting cloud. Many wisdom teachers have proposed reasons why integration is difficult, and why we need conscious attention, intention, and deep reflection to truly integrate what we learn, and change according to our new knowledge.

This integration may be difficult because we tend to activate only part of our bodies, minds, and spirits in the endeavor—we have been socialized to think our way through every problem and ignore other powerful modes of learning. We also value speed in our fast-paced lives and do not allow enough time to reflect upon and integrate all of our life experiences, so many opportunities for powerful learning are lost. Even when we have free time, we tend to fill it up with distractions that prevent us from true integration. Integration begins with reflection on our current experiences and figuring out how our experiences fit with our past, and whether our current responses serve us well or could use some changes.

Reflection

"Look deep into nature, and then you will understand everything better." (Albert Einstein)

The word reflection comes from the Latin, "the act of bending back." We look into a mirror to see our images reflected back to us. In our contemporary times, reflection means finding space and time in our lives to get away from the distractions of everyday life and process more deeply. Angeles Arrien (*Second Half of Life*) noted that reflection is a tool used in all world traditions to review, question, and reassess our life experiences. Where better to reflect on life experiences than at the beach? The water on a still calm sunny day reflects sunlight and acts as a mirror. At other times, in other illumination, the surface of the ocean absorbs the harsh light, taking away the emotional baggage of our experience and leaving only the softer essence of the lesson. When the surf is pounding a sandy beach, the water mixes with the sand in a thick grainy mess. It resembles much of our life experience, with the meaning obscured by the muck.

We need patience for the lessons to come to us, but we also need to make a rigorous practice of "bending back" our busy schedules to create time for reflection. I think of reflection as the container in which integration work can occur. Reflection is the process of looking into the mirror with a corresponding willingness to really see what is there. It involves an opening up that allows shifts in perspective, new ideas, answers to problems, and new insights to arise. Some people call this process contemplation. But as my experience with the insights recorded in my journal reveal, reflection alone is not sufficient to make positive changes in one's life. Reflection is often a heady process—one of thinking. For things to change, the insights prompted by reflection need to be integrated throughout the heart, mind, and guts, and need to result in some changes in behavior or perspective.

I think of reflection as the process of identifying all of the pieces of the puzzle and metaphorically laying them out on the table. We might have one middle piece, the current problem or event, but surrounding it are all the other pieces that fit together to make the big picture. These other pieces are past experiences with similar problems, patterns in our behavior or the behavior of others, fragmented memories, expectations, assumptions, judgments, feelings, and a host of other components. The single piece of the puzzle that represents the current problem only gives us a glimpse of what the final picture will be. Often, we have to find those corner pieces that anchor the big picture before we can make headway. So reflection is the gathering of all these pieces and laying them out for our consideration. Integration is the assembling of the puzzle—using our cognitive, emotional, spiritual, and other resources to find the big picture that integrates body, mind, and spirit. We know when we have found the big picture because we feel an alignment of head, heart, and gut and the puzzle pieces now make sense. If we think we have an answer, but feel somewhat doubtful (half-hearted) or have a gut-level reaction, we are not yet in alignment and need more reflection time. We might be missing a crucial piece or have forced a piece into a slot where it does not belong. So how do we use all of our gifts, talents, and resources to integrate our experience and cultivate wisdom? In our too busy, fast-paced lives, it is no wonder that we seem not to learn from our mistakes and thus, are doomed to repeat them. Reflection takes time.

Integration

"Last night I drifted into a sense of deep belonging, and the awareness that I am the World. It's so easy to get lost in thinking about the experience, but when there is a moment of identity there's no mistaking it...I've been at it for many years, and still have only rare moments of integration. Most of the time, I still experience the natural world as a mere backdrop to my individual activity." (Robert Kull, Solitude, p. 138)

Science is beginning to study this process of integration and explore how our bodies, minds, and spirits work together to solve problems, as well as how we integrate the internal and external worlds. One of the contemporary integrative thinkers was Dr. Candace Pert (*Molecules of Emotion*), a western laboratory scientist known in the scientific world for discovering the opiate receptor in the brain. This finding, in the 1970s, shed light on how addictive substances act on the brain. She found that substances circulating in the bloodstream can only affect us if we have receptors on our cells to identify the substance. We all have opiate receptors, and people use opiates because they relieve pain and they create a sensation of bliss and/or expanded consciousness. Scientists soon discovered that our bodies produce an opiate substance naturally as well. We call those substances endorphins.

This finding was big, but what came later was even bigger, from the integration of body and mind perspective. Dr. Pert found these opiate receptors were not just located in the brain, but were on cells throughout the entire body, particularly in clusters in the immune system. She found that these opiate receptors have a central role in our emotional responses. These cells in the immune system and throughout the body have the capacity to learn, can regulate mood, and hold memories—activities we used to think were limited to the mind or the brain. It turns out that emotions are recorded and regulated throughout the whole body—we are an integrated bodymind system, as traditional Chinese medicine has known for centuries. There are concentrations of these receptor sites everywhere where we take in sensory information, meaning that all incoming information is filtered through our memories of past experiences and the emotions associated with those memories. The body automatically undertakes an integration process, but often we halt the process by suppressing emotion or triggering negative thoughts that interfere with true integration.

A major message of this research is that we cannot heal or cure ourselves of maladies through thought alone—mind over matter--or through biochemical manipulations alone. Instead, we need to feel with our whole bodies in order to heal. We talk about having "gut reactions" or being "heartsick" and it turns out those things are literally true. There are concentrations of opiate receptor cells in the intestines and around the heart. Music, scents, tastes, and places may activate memories that are located deep in our bodies rather than in our brains. These memories may not have words attached to them, like most of the memories stored in the brain do. This deep body wisdom is often dismissed because our western science has separated body from mind, and has chosen to label the mind as the place of thinking and wisdom, and the body as automatic functions such as breathing and swallowing, or as a passive thing controlled by the brain. Here is an explanation for my experience of a vague "upset." My body is reacting to some event without benefit of the brain's words. I feel it in my gut, but cannot explain it readily. What we call intuition may also be an example of body memory and wisdom.

Another integrative thinker is Ken Wilber, whose "theory of everything" offers a broad map to synthesize all knowledge about human experience (see for example, *Integral Spirituality*, *Integral Psychology*, or the more accessible, *The Integral Life Vision*, for more detail). His four quadrant theory is a useful way of organizing the vast amount of knowledge from western science as well as eastern, western, and indigenous philosophy and ancient wisdom traditions. Wilber shows how focusing on only one quadrant of influence, or only one type of knowledge, is limiting. For example, focusing only on the tide tables to judge the size of waves, and ignoring season, winds, weather events and other factors, means that I might get swept away by high surf. To truly integrate our experiences, we have to understand the big picture. Imagine that you have divided a piece of paper into four equal compartments or quadrants. In a nutshell, the four quadrants outline the influence of:

- ❖ The upper right box contains information about our physical bodies and their products (hormones, neurotransmitters, movements, disorders and diseases, etc),
- ❖ The upper left box includes the inner life of the individual, such as thoughts, emotions, intelligence, states of consciousness, spirituality, and all the stages or phases of individual development,
- ❖ The lower left box is the immediate socio-cultural environment composed of our families, neighborhoods, schools, peers, religious or spiritual leaders and organizations, and local communities, and
- ❖ The lower right box contains the broader societal level influences, such as legal issues, the media, religious doctrines, systems of government, politics, educational institutions, geopolitical formations, historical events and trends, and so on.

The two upper quadrants represent our individual influences—our insides and outsides; and the two lower quadrants are external influences—those close to us, and those more distal. So to understand why my past intimate relationships have not worked, I have to consider the possible contributions from all four quadrants. From the upper right quadrant factors, I can ask myself: Am I biochemically or evolutionarily hard-wired to have trouble committing? Am I attracted to certain people because of their pheromones with no conscious control? I hate that thought—I do not want to be a "slave" to my biology. I need another explanation for why am I immediately drawn to certain people but grow to be attracted to others over time.

From the upper left quadrant, I can ask myself: What role have my past experiences had on my thinking and feeling about relationships? What expectations have I created? Did my personality or stage of development match or complement my partner, or were we at very different phases of life? Was I being myself (authentic) in this relationship or masking/hiding my true self? Did something in my nature or behavior draw a certain kind of person?

From the lower left quadrant: What did I learn about relationships from my family? At school? How have my peers contributed to my expectations about relationships? What did I learn from observing my parents, and the parents of friends? What role has my spiritual development played in relationships? How much did my stoic Scandinavian upbringing influence my conflict avoidance?

Finally, from the lower right quadrant: How has the media contributed to my unrealistic views of relationships? What about the fact that I was not legally allowed to marry my same-sex partners? Did religious doctrines against same-sex relationships affect me on a subconscious level, dooming my relationships to fail? Did religious expectations about sex and love and the obligation to raise a family affect me more than I thought? Did I internalize shame and guilt about sex?

This model can be applied to any life problem, or to any aspect of one's own growth and development. Why am I shy? Why do I feel depressed and what should I do about it? Why am I so attached to a particular identity? In addition to these quadrant questions, I can consider different ways of knowing that are attached to each quadrant. Western science resides mostly in the upper right quadrant, and is only one way of knowing. Buddhism values direct experience of one's own internal processes (an upper left quadrant activity), as does western psychotherapy. In the past, I have valued science over my own direct experience, but I have also been unduly influenced by the romantic stories in the popular media. If I am mulling over a problem in the lower left quadrant of relationships, I may need to apply ethnographic methods of careful observation over time to solve the problem. And those lower right quadrant influences need methods such as systems or chaos theories or spiral dynamics to understand how they work.

These days, whenever I am mulling over a new problem, I often "map out" the problem in the four quadrants, and I always gain more insight from the activity. It helps me to identify the areas where I have some choice, and the places that are beyond my control. It also helps me to know that there are different tools for understanding different kinds of problems.

Angeles Arrien (*IndepthYearlong*) has some very practical advice for facilitating the integration of life's experiences. She observed that we often get caught up in telling the story of some past event. That story has a plot, fascinating characters, and high drama. Sometimes we find ourselves stuck in the telling of a story because the story gets us attention, sympathy, or validation, all of which reinforce the story. The next time we embellish it a bit to further the effect. What if we leave the story behind and focus on what we learned from the experience instead? These little nuggets of knowledge are the foundation for integration and deeper understanding, not the stories themselves.

I took this lesson to heart one rainy afternoon, and reviewed old journals that told the stories of my past relationships. Only the week before this discussion of stories in Angeles' group, I had lamented to a friend that I seemed to have learned nothing from these experiences, even though I had hundreds of pages of journal entries processing the relationships, particularly their beginnings and endings. Notably, there were big gaps in my journaling when things were going well—I was not documenting what worked. How could I figure out how to improve my relationships if I did not track both—what went wrong (missteps) and what went right?

The journals were full of compelling and dramatic stories and focused on how I felt about or reacted to some event, but there was no deeper processing or integration of the experiences. I devoted the next hour to writing the two or three main lessons I had learned from each intimate relationship of my adult life. The final result was about three pages, as compared to about 300 pages of stories. In those succinct three pages were the kernels of wisdom that I needed to integrate. The types of knowledge contained in those nuggets were informed by my understanding of Ken Wilber's four-quadrant model, and therefore, so much more comprehensive than a list of lessons that focused only on the interpersonal aspects of relationships. These are the raw materials to take to the beach for reflection.

Moving from Integration to Action

"I've always placed great value on insights, but in some sense they're a dime a dozen. They come and they go. I long for understanding and wisdom, but no longer know what I'm seeking. If all is transient, including clarity and peace, then what is there to seek? ...I still have no idea what my soul is. There are thoughts, emotions, physical sensations, and though Buddhism says it's an illusion—a sense of I, but what is the soul?" (Robert Kull, Solitude, p. 95)

Wisdom is of no value if it is not put into action or shared. All the good thoughts in the world are useless if not implemented. Robert Kull pointed out some of the reasons that we do not implement wisdom—we have flashes of insight that seem profound, but they fade quickly and we are left with doubts about what they mean. We may fail to follow up on the insight if we allow our old ego mechanisms and cognitive distortions to kick in gear. How often have we have had a profound experience, and then moved into second-guessing or questioning our experience later?

"Vision without action is a daydream.
Action without vision is a nightmare."
(Japanese Proverb)

Journaling is one of the oldest and most useful tools for tracking our insights and the lessons learned in life. How else will we identify our patterns and gain the insight to change them? A journal can be used to record insights, but more than that, reflect on them and integrate them into our daily experience so the insight results in a change in perception and/or behavior. We have so many thoughts in any given day, that the insights and lessons of the day can easily be lost if we do not track and record them. Journaling is a tool for reflection and integration, but is not action. In a journal, we can record our insights, and we can track our efforts to change our behavior, and what happens when we change. However, there is a danger that the journal becomes a place to tell, rehash, and embellish our stories. We need conscious effort to keep our journals "true," and to initiate changes in our everyday lives.

The journal can be a great place to track our efforts to change and record the effects of those life changes, as long as writing is not a substitute for action. For example, as I started this project, I had a misguided idea that I would "write myself into wisdom." Indeed, I have had many insights along the way, but unless I put those insights into practice in my daily life, the book becomes inauthentic ramblings—the daydream of vision without action. My challenge is to live the principles that I outline by incorporating my insights into actions.

Going Deeper
1. Reflect on the quote from John Muir below. Have you had that experience of intending just to take a walk, but finding yourself going deep within yourself and accessing deeper knowledge?
   "I only went out for a walk and finally concluded to stay out til sundown, for going out, I found, was really going in." (John Muir)
2. Think of a recent traumatic event in your life. Instead of retelling the story, write about what you learned from the experience in a one-page vignette. The first paragraph describes the essence of the event without the gory details or analysis; just the facts. The second paragraph focuses on what you learned from the experience. End by giving gratitude to the person or event that taught you this powerful lesson.
3. Start a new journal solely for the purpose of recording lessons learned and tracking changes in your behavior. Resist the attraction of writing out the stories. If you feel you need to record the stories, use a diary or a different journal than you use to track behavior and lessons.
4. Below is a four-quadrant map for thinking about life problems. Use it to consider a problem in your own life at this time.

Using the Four Quadrants to Understand Life's Problems

Inner Life of the Individual: Mind, Spirit What are my emotions, thoughts, or spiritual reactions about the issue? What are the roles and identities that I am most attached to at this time? Where am I developmentally? Do I have shadow issues to work on (negative ego processes like pride, attachment, fears of abandonment, conflict avoidance) or areas of my self-hood that are less well-developed? What is my predominant worldview at this time?	**Outer Aspects of the Individual: The Body** How is my physical body involved in this issue? Where do I experience this issue (in my head, heart, or gut or elsewhere)? Do I need professional help, such as from a health care provider, acupuncturist, body worker, to deal with the physical aspects of the problem? Do I need to change my diet, sleep patterns, or other aspects that affect my physical body?
The Immediate Socio-Cultural Influences What are the influences on this current problem from my immediate social environment, such as my: • family, • significant other, • neighborhood, • communities, • coworkers, • local religious/spiritual communities? •	**The Societal Arena** How does the broader society, world economy, politics, laws, media, historical time period, religious doctrines, and so on, impact this issue?

9
Solitude

"Vocation to solitude is to deliver oneself up, to hand oneself over, to trust completely to the silence of a wide landscape of woods and hills, or sea and desert." (Thomas Merton, Dialogues with Silence)

    I like nothing better than walking on a long stretch of beach without another person in sight. I relish the solitude at this stage of my life, and in fact, I crave it. What is solitude? The dictionary definition refers to being alone or being lonely, with two distinctions. Isolation is being shut out from others or the world whereas seclusion is typically a voluntary shutting out of the world or other people for a period of time. Philosophers and ancient and contemporary wisdom teachers have a different definition that has nothing to do with loneliness. They always recommend seeking solitude as a state of being that enhances deep reflection and inner knowing. That is, solitude is a desirable state of being alone for the purpose of personal growth work.

    Loneliness is an uncomfortable state of being and a feeling of lack that is often not helped by being with people. This fact points out that being alone and being lonely are two quite distinct experiences. Loneliness is a state of unrest within the individual that cannot be cured by solely seeking out company, but by making a shift in our inner world to find comfortable company with ourselves. So, solitude is not the same as merely being alone, or lonely, but is an exercise in reducing the distractions from other people and facilitating a focus inward on our own personal growth and wellbeing. Solitude enhances integration, and ironically, solitude can be a cure for loneliness. We can be alone and fill up our body-minds with distractions like watching TV, playing video games, reading non-enlightening books, having negative daydreams, and so on. These are activities that do not promote character development. They are not necessarily bad things to do—we all need some down-time or distraction from time to time. However, when we have important personal growth work to do, we need productive solitude; a date with oneself that leads to deeper integration of knowledge and ultimately, wisdom.

In this section, I will describe beachwise solitude as a conscious emptying of the mind with a simultaneous engagement of the senses that allows thoughts or feelings to arise at will, a process that can be focused on specific problem-solving or one particular issue, but may also render us open to whatever messages may manifest. Think for a moment about how different our beach experiences can be. One day, we take a beach stroll with a good friend and focus on the social aspect of being with the friend. We enjoy the sun and the surf, but our focus is outward—on the relationship with the friend. Another day, we walk alone on a deserted beach, and let the wind and the waves take us inward for contemplation. We need solitude in order to see the world in a different perspective, one that is more detached and objective.

Solitude and Maturation

"And I can be content again in the solitude of the sand,
Graduated by the wind and respected by the sea-world."
(Pablo Neruda)

Solitude, particularly in nature, appears to facilitate healthy growth as a spiritual being. Joseph Krutch (*The Voice of the Desert*) suggested that if we do not know nature, we cannot know ourselves, and if we do not know ourselves, we cannot know others. Solitude combined with nature seems to be a potent combination for developing wisdom.

Anne Morrow Lindberg described solitude as a tool for considering our own growth and development first, apart from the other people in our life. She said, *"Woman must come of age by herself."* This the only section of *Gift from the Sea* that I initially found difficult to relate to and that felt dated. The life experience of women sixty years ago was much different than today. I have never been a wife or a mother. I grew up with second wave feminism to inform my adolescence and young adulthood, and I knew from a very early age that I did not want to follow the path of my mother, as much as I loved and respected my mother. I always knew that I would have to take care of myself, and my adult life has been characterized by relatively long periods of solitude—both the lonely kind and the reflective kind. But I do know that many women, perhaps more so than men, have difficulty finding time for reflective solitude in their lives and are challenged if they try to put their own needs ahead of the needs of others. Lindbergh wrote about women of her generation,

> *"she has swung between these two opposite poles of dependence and competition, of Victorianism and Feminism. Both extremes throw her off balance, neither is the center, the true center of being a woman"* (p. 96).

I bristled at that statement, knowing that it was feminism that led me to recognize competition and aggression as unhealthy practices that stemmed from a western, patriarchal value system that I could denounce or at least resist in my own life. Feminism was, and is, part of my center, and I found supportive groups of women throughout my personal and professional lives to nourish my soul and help me understand my experiences as a woman in the world. Feminism led me into social justice work in my community. Then I took a deep breath and let Anne Morrow Lindbergh's experience be what it was; her own experience in a different time in history, and deep with wisdom about the need for solitude. When I did that, I could see how those old ideas about women are still in play today, albeit in more subtle forms. I could relate to the need for solitude to reflect about the complexities of negotiating relationships, and for forging deeper self-knowing.

The stereotype that women should place other people's needs ahead of their own has created some conflicts in my own intimate relationships. In some instances, I have been accused of being selfish when I asserted my needs and refused to compromise on issues that I felt were essential to my own integrity and wellbeing. In the past, I sometimes felt guilty about these events, but on retrospect, I am satisfied that I made the right choices in most of these situations. If I had given in to the demands or requests of partners, I would have given up chunks of my own integrity and authenticity. Many of these conflicts were over my need for solitude, which I usually expressed as a need for "space." Nothing in our culture encourages solitude, particularly solitude in nature, so some of my partners felt I was choosing myself or nature, over them. Our culture pushes us to constant social interaction, labeling this sociality as "normal," and not recognizing the value of solitude to enhance our relationships.

Solitude provides the space in which to process relationship issues, as well as one's own nature. To me, the equation reads: Solitude plus reflection equals integration and groundedness. When my partners asserted that my need for solitude was proof that I did not love them, I tried to explain that I could be a better partner if I had regular times for solitude. I am a slow processer of emotional exchanges, and cannot really understand the underlying dynamics of a relationship problem at the time it is unfolding. I need to take those issues to nature in solitude to reflect and process.

In one relationship, my partner wanted immediate answers and was never satisfied when I asked for time alone to think about the issue. Because my requests for solitude went unheard, I tried to create alone time for myself—in warm weather, I got up at five am to work in the garden, knowing I would have at least two hours to myself. I created an office for myself in the back corner of the basement where my partner hated to go. But to this partner, love meant spending all our waking hours together. Ultimately, the fact that my partner had a different perspective on solitude and connection than I did, and her constant violations of my boundaries, resulted in the end of that relationship. I could not give up solitude without compromising my integrity.

Solitude and Connection

"Nobody with me at sea but myself." (Oliver Goldsmith)

Solitude in nature often leads to a sense of connection with the cosmos. Separating ourselves from typical human relationships can open us to sense that the sea and the earth are our peers or parents or higher power. Nature is in us and of us, and it brings peace, contentment, gratitude, and inspiration.

On the deserted beach, walking in solitude, I experience at first the illusion of being alone. There is a certain thrill, a lightening of my heart, when I gaze ahead and see only sand and water stretching into the horizon. But once I open my senses to the experience, I notice multitudes of birds, wheeling in the air above me, plunging in the water to reappear with a silver flash of fish in their beaks, or popping in and out of sight as they float on the waves. They screech, squawk, pip, or caw over the roar of the ocean. If I focus my sight just beyond the break of the waves, I may see seals, sea lions, sea otters, dolphins, and a host of unknown fish that briefly breech the surface. If I am lucky, I may spot a migrating whale. If I find myself on a rocky shore, the rocks are covered in living beings: barnacles, mussels, limpets, crabs, anemones, and snails. These are the tip of the iceberg, the creatures I can see if I pay attention. When I walk the beach early in the morning at low tide, the sand is criss-crossed with tracks of sea creatures—worms, insects, and mole crabs that leave these traces but remain hidden from sight. The beachfront and the ocean teams with unseen, microscopic life, but they put no demands on my attention, so I can feel alone and yet connected at the same time.

Why do we tend to limit our acquaintance to other humans? So much can be learned from befriending the creatures in and around the sea. I tend to think of the ocean itself as a living, breathing organism, an idea considered science fiction by much of our culture. The ocean has "moods," some days calm, other days agitated or angry, and many times, joyous. The ocean has different looks, different smells, and different feels from day to day.

We ascribe consciousness only to human beings, but since we can hardly even define what we mean by consciousness in ourselves, why are we so arrogant as to assume that other beings are not conscious? Once I was sitting by the waterfront as the Blue Angels navy jets practiced for an air show. The water was filled with seals, more than I had ever seen at once at this particular spot along Crissy Field. Every time the jets flew overhead, emitting that deafening sonic boom, the heads popped out of the water, looking around. The seals did not appear to be frightened, but rather, to be curious. They were splashing and cavorting in the water as if they were enjoying the air show as much as the humans on the shore. I saw intelligence and consciousness in the curious brown eyes of the seal. Feeling alone is an illusion, created by the human mind, and the experience of solitude can lead us to transform loneliness into sacred solitude and connection with earth and cosmos.

Robert Kull (*Solitude*) spent a year on a remote island in Patagonia to study the effects of solitude on his own development. He noted,

> *"In solitude I'm released from the immediate tangle of the social web and free to explore other levels of existence. I have the opportunity to relax and experience myself as part of the rhythms of nature."* (p. 80)

When he returned to civilization and reflected on his experience, he reported that he experienced a depression, partly related to his feeling that he had not returned with any big answers. But upon further reflection, he had experienced an expansion of space and time, and he had lived by nature's rhythms of tides, season, sun and moon, rather than a watch. His senses had been awakened, he felt more alive and connected, and he gained a greater understanding of the grip that the need to feel in control holds over our lives. He began to comprehend just how difficult it is to surrender control and trust in other people or circumstances. He found that even in absence of other people, his interpersonal difficulties played out. A cat triggered his frustration and anger when the cat crossed his boundaries or requested too much attention. He raged at the wind, at first feeling it a personal affront to his comfort.

The lesson for me after reading his book was that we all struggle with these same lessons. I do not want to spend a year in solitude if I can learn the same lessons from my own daily experiences. Wisdom may be harder to acquire with the competing demands of everyday life, but if I build regular periods of solitude into my everyday routine, I can reap the benefits. Kull's experiences help me to understand that I might not find the "ultimate" answers, but that ongoing integration of my experience through reflection and solitude will deepen my wisdom. Wisdom is not a concrete thing to achieve, but a lifelong process.

Silence

"Let us look for secret things somewhere in the world on the blue shore of silence." (Pablo Neruda)

One of the values of spending time in solitude in nature is the experience of silence. In our everyday lives, we are surrounded by unnatural noise; traffic, construction, fire engine sirens, dogs barking, music blaring from cars as they pass by, conversations of other people on the bus and in restaurants, or the neighbor's TV or stereo. Most of all, there is that incessant chatter in our own heads, the internal voice that never shuts up. Nature is full of sound as well, but in solitude, the absence of the unnatural sounds allows us to hear the natural—wind rustling the grasses, the singing sands, roaring waves, tree branches creaking in the wind, and the multitude of different bird calls. These natural sounds promote a sense of inner stillness. Mark Coleman (*Alive in the Wild*) noted that *"silence is the doorway to the mystery, to the sacred. It is in silence that we can feel the essence of things"* (p. 148).

Most religious and spiritual traditions value silence as the doorway to the sacred, as access to the soul. One of the proverbs in the old testament Bible noted, "closing one's lips makes a person wise." Silence allows us to access the inner world, without the noisy distractions of the outer world. Sometimes we recognize that silence is sacred when we "take a moment of silence" to remember a person we lost or some tragic event. But silence is a rare commodity in today's world.

In *A Square Inch of Silence*, Gordon Hempton, an acoustic ecologist, recounted his search for natural silence in the United States. He studied the impact of noise on human and animal life, finding evidence of the devastating effect of man-made noise. For example, the increase in ambient noise has been particularly hard on songbirds, because they must sing louder, thus expending more energy, and making them more vulnerable to predators. At least one-fourth of all bird species in the U.S. are on the decline. Dolphins in China's Yantze River are nearly extinct, mostly because of the noise of shipping traffic. In 2007, then president Bush overrode scientific concern about the navy's use of sonar and exempted the navy from two major environmental laws and a federal court decision, meant to protect marine mammals.

In humans, noise pollution is associated with higher levels of aggression and a decline in helping behavior toward others. Road traffic noise has been linked to cardiovascular disease. There are over 5000 research articles that show detrimental effects of noise, likening it to second hand smoke. Hempton's travels revealed only a handful of places in the entire U.S. with natural quiet, defined as an interval of more than fifteen minutes without an intrusion of man-made noise. Our national parks have only about five minute intervals of natural quiet during daylight hours. Silence should be on the endangered list along with the California condor.

Sometimes when I go to a remote beach, I prepare myself on the way. I do not turn on the radio, or think about what is happening in my life at the time. Instead, I set intentions: *"I am going to the beach to learn what the beach has to offer me today."* I try to stay present with driving, and with noticing the beauty of the landscape. At first, even the sound of the engine bothers me, but soon, I get into a "zone." Angeles Arrien called it the *"sweet territory of silence."* When I get to the beach, I listen to the sound of my own breathing on the inside, and the sound of the waves outside, and soon they synchronize. Now I am ready to receive the blessings from the beach, and all the wondrous and varied sounds become distinguishable, a veritable symphony of nature's sounds. Rumi must have experienced this wonder of nature sounds, leading him to exclaim: *"We have fallen into the place where everything is music."*

Going Deeper
1. How much time have you allotted in your life to solitude? How much of that is in nature? What lessons have you learned from periods of solitude?
2. If you are like most people, you do not have sufficient time in solitude. Develop a plan that gradually increases the amount of time you commit to solitude, and make it a sacred, non-negotiable time in your life.
3. Have you incorporated periods of silence into your daily routine? What benefits do you derive from silence? If you have not yet experienced a conscious, extended period of silence, try it for a day, or whatever amount of time is feasible for you.
4. Consider this quote from Rumi. What does it mean to you?

    "Silence is the sea, and speech is like the river. The sea is seeking you: don't seek the river. Don't turn your head away from the signs offered by the sea."

5. Rilke is one of the most prolific and poetic writers about solitude. What are your reactions to Rilke's ideas about solitude?

"What is necessary, after all, is only this: solitude, vast inner solitude. To walk inside of yourself and meet no one for hours -- that is what you must be able to attain."

"Love consists in this, that two solitudes protect and touch and greet each other."

10
Cycles of Life

"Is it not possible that middle age can be looked upon as a...second adolescence?...The signs that presage growth, so similar, it seems to me, to those in early adolescence: discontent, restlessness, doubt, despair, longing, are interpreted as signs of decay...in middle age, because of the false assumption that it is a period of decline, one interprets these life-signs, paradoxically, as signs of approaching death. Instead of facing them, one runs away; one escapes—into depressions, nervous breakdowns, drink, love affairs, or frantic, thoughtless fruitless overwork. Anything rather than face them. Anything rather than stand still and learn from them."
(Anne Morrow Lindbergh, 1955, pp. 86-87)

Beaches are strewn with the reminders of the cycles of life and death. There are translucent heaps of dead jellyfish, whitened pieces of driftwood that were once living, breathing trees, remains of tiny creatures plucked from their hiding places in the sand by sea gulls. The white sand dollar is a skeleton, bleached white by the sun long after its life as a furry purple being ceased. Why do so many humans pass by these signs of life and death everyday and yet fail to recognize their own mortality? Maybe we are drawn to the beach because it embodies the spirit of youth, of renewal. As Robert and Seon Manley (*Beaches, their lives, legend, and lore*) noted, *"Nearly every beach is young. The rest of the world can be hoary with age, arrogant with its old mountains, mysterious with old seas; but the beach is ever young, ever renewed"* (p. 21).

Beaches are not actually young, they are instead continually re-created by wind, waves, and tides, and embody the perfect blend of old and new. When old materials are shuffled around and re-constituted, they create something new and wondrous. How can we use this concept of re-creation and renewal in our own lives as we age? Can we take advantage of the tides of life to re-arrange our old parts and incorporate new learning that washes up on the shore of our existence, and stay young in heart and spirit if not in physical body?

My reaction to the changes of mid life came as a complete shock to me. For more than ten years, I had been teaching courses about aging, and routinely told my students that midlife adults often had intense fears about death and dying, ruminated over their mortality, and engaged in serious re-appraisals of their lives. Apparently I thought I was exempt from this process. My father's death when I was 44, plunged me into a ten-year cycle of "midlife crisis," and my developmental psychology background was little consolation and no practical help. Nowhere in our culture is there any encouragement to *"stand still and learn"* as Anne Morrow Lindberg suggested, no fostering of our own direct experiences with maturation. Instead, we are urged to stay young at all costs and to avoid talking to each other about death or aging. I escaped, as Anne Morrow Lindbergh put it so well, into *"Frantic, thoughtless, fruitless, overwork."*

Ripening or Rotting?

"Alone, alone, all alone, alone on a wide wide sea!
And never a saint took pity on my soul in agony."
(Samuel Taylor Coleridge, Rime of the Ancient Mariner)

Angeles Arrien's beautiful and profound book, *The Second Half of Life*, offers a blueprint for negotiating midlife and older adulthood, using the visual image of gates or portals that must be traveled on the way to healthy elder wisdom. She noted that in contemporary society,

> *"we have forgotten the rites of passage that help us learn to become wise elders who actively participate in our communities and live deep, fulfilling lives. Unfortunately, our cultures' current perspective is that the second half of life offers only decline, disease, despair, and death."* (p. 1)

Oh, how I could relate to that statement and the quote from Anne Morrow Lindberg that begins this chapter. As my "midlife crisis" reached a peak a few years after my father's death, I saw only a long road of decline ahead of me. I observed so many contradictions. Whereas many of my students and colleagues seemed to look to me for wisdom (which I did not feel), other young strangers seemed not to see me at all. As a middle-aged woman, I was beginning to feel invisible, overlooked in my culture. Media images favored young, anorexic women, and older women figured only as mothers or grandmothers, neither of which I could relate to very much. If I was out of my role as professor, I became largely invisible. Clerks in stores did not appear to see me waiting patiently at the counter and young people ran into me on the street, or pushed me aside as I tried to mount the steps to the bus.

But most importantly, I did not feel "wise" in my own conduct. I knew a lot of "facts" that led to a perception of wisdom in the classroom or my profession, but in my personal life, I was repeating old patterns and not learning from my mistakes. In other words, I was getting older, but not wiser, stuck in an adolescent-like state of wondering who I was and who I was becoming.

It was only a few years ago that I first read Carl Jung, a scholar distained by the psychology department in which I studied. Jung, in *Stages of Life*, suggested that an inner process typically begins between ages 35 and 40, whereby people start to shed their youthful illusions and let repressed childhood dreams emerge. This is a time of increased wisdom and a search for personal values. Jung suggested that if we do not initiate this process, we stay in an adolescent, self-centered mode of being and stagnate.

Angeles Arrien graciously allows a few more years to act the self-centered adolescent than did Jung. She tells us that after age 50, to act in ways that are not guided by wisdom is to be "less than becoming." I sought guidance from wisdom teachers about how to age with dignity and foster the development of wisdom. One thing I discovered is that an important task of maturation is to acknowledge, confront, and integrate the shadow sides of my ego—all of those undesirable thoughts and characteristics that I have spent a lifetime so far denying, repressing, or projecting on others. Thomas Moore (*Care of the Soul*) noted "*the uniqueness of a person is made up of the insane and the twisted as much as it is of the rational and normal.*" I have discovered that shadows are not always negative things. I might have very positive qualities or gifts and talents that I have not owned. For example, I thought that I had lost my sense of humor during that ten-year period of transition, and did not recognize it was back until several people told me how funny I was. I finally reclaimed my dry wit as one of my strengths, and low and behold, it flourished and I started writing humor stories.

I have many shadow characteristics to deal with, both good and bad, but one that I have encountered much lately is pride. I have struggled with identifying the line between healthy pride and self-confidence, which consists of satisfaction with doing something well, and unhealthy pride, which often slips into arrogance and a sense of entitlement. Unhealthy pride often arises out of judgments and comparing myself to others. I can see how not addressing these shadow characteristics can lead to a "rotting" of my soul rather than a ripening into wisdom. Luckily, I still have time. According to Angeles Arrien (*Second Half of Life*), midlife is about gaining perspective, and older age is about wisdom. She noted that "*wisdom is a process, not an outcome*" (p. 139), so I am happy to be at the beginning of this process as I leave behind the transition in chronological years from midlife to older adulthood. I am happy to be in the youth of my elder years now. With the help of the beach, I might yet achieve some level of maturity and wisdom if I start to seriously address the shadow sides of my nature.

When I am walking on the beach, if the sun is behind me, my shadow is cast in front of me. It might be very short if the sun is high in the sky, or quite elongated if the sun is low in the sky. If I am walking into the sun, my shadow is behind me, invisible unless I consciously turn around to see it. If it is overcast or foggy, I will not be able to see my shadow at all. So metaphorically, I can walk with my back to the sun so that my shadow stays within my view. I can remind myself that in times of confusion, the shadow may be working me behind the scenes. I may need to cast a light upon it so it doesn't do too much damage. I can become accustomed to my shadow, examine it, and eventually, befriend it as it walks before me in life. It is my daily companion, so I may as well integrate it so it doesn't continue to affect my behavior from behind the scenes.

Wising Up

"I need the sea because it teaches me.
I don't know if I learn music or awareness,
If it's a single wave or its vast existence…
The fact is that until I fall asleep,
In some magnetic way I move in
The university of the waves." (Pablo Neruda)

So, how does one go about acquiring wisdom, to matriculating into the "university of the waves"? Is wisdom tied to age and cycles of life? Most western theorists seem to think so, because wisdom seems to come from having a broader view of life, and the integration of life's experiences. The more life experience, the more material one has to reflect upon, identify patterns, and integrate. According to Erik Erikson, midlife is a time of generativity, or giving back to the world, a sharing of one's gifts and talents, and older age is the prime time for the development of wisdom. The more life experience we have, the greater the possibility for deep integration that we can share with others and that fosters the growth of wisdom.

Angeles Arrien suggested that people who are age 50 and older face four frontiers:

- ❖ Retirement
- ❖ Being a mentor, steward, and/or grandparent
- ❖ Coping with an aging body
- ❖ Facing mortality

As I transitioned across the country in my early 50s, and started to awaken, I realized that facing mortality as my father was dying, had triggered my midlife crisis at a much deeper more personal level than had any reading or thinking about death and dying I had done as a teacher. That earlier reading was a cognitive activity, and my father's death was a complex experience that touched me at all levels—physical, emotional, cognitive, and spiritual. It was also an interpersonal experience shared by my mother, siblings, other relatives, and family friends, all of whom had their own perspectives on death and dying. I needed (and still need) deep work around issues of mortality. I want to find some level of peace about the process of aging and dying. This, I find from my reading, is one of the major developmental tasks or transitions of midlife and older adult development. Because of this introspection on death and dying prompted by my father's death, 15 years later when my mother was diagnosed with a recurrence of breast cancer, spread to her bones, I was able to support her in a very different way than I had been with my father.

With my father, I had focused on trying to help him "beat the disease," because I did not accept that he was dying. But when my mother called and left a message to call her back because she had something to tell me, I knew immediately that she was dying. I accepted the diagnosis of recurrent cancer instead of denying it. Instead of "beating the disease," I became intent on listening to my mother's wishes and needs and honoring them. I spent more quality time with her, encouraging her to re-tell the story of her life (which was the story of my life as well). I was mostly ok with her gallows humor, of her asking me to take her on her "goodbye tour" across the state to visit old friends and family once more. The hardest part of the whole experience was her explicitly stated request that I be her "rock." She wanted me to treat her "normally" without tears, overt expressions of grief, clinging, or any sign that I was aware that she was dying. That was so ironic, given that a few years earlier I had moved away so I could learn to be more expressive and show my feelings to others. Now, when I was with my mother, I had to revert back to my stoic upbringing. It took a toll. On nearly every trip to visit her, I would cry in the rental car during the entire 45 minute drive back to the airport. I had to release the pain of holding those feelings in for days or weeks at a time. I had the privilege and honor of holding her hand through the last days and hours of her life, along with my siblings and witness her passing. The last few weeks of her life were particularly hard, as she regressed into a person I did not know, but my work with Angeles and my beach practices had given me tools that helped me stay with the pain and the grief and not want to flee.

So where does one go to find a sense of peace around the prospect of dying? My parents both had a solid religious belief in an afterlife that comforted them. I don't have that. My scientific, rational mind resists the concept of taking things on faith. I have considered different religious views on what happens after death of the physical body, but they do not bring me comfort. I was raised in a protestant Christian faith with its concepts of heaven and hell, but the older I get, the more suspicious I am of this dualistic idea of permanent location. Hardly anyone is all bad or all good, so what ratio of good to bad is necessary to get into heaven? If you do just one really bad thing, but otherwise lead a good life, will you go to hell? It seems way too simplistic. I was not raised with the idea of purgatory, but that makes more sense, since most of human beings are somewhere in the middle of the continuum between good and bad. Purgatory must be a very crowded place. If there is a heaven on earth, then surely that place must be a sandy beach. Re-incarnation does not appeal to me either, since I am so firmly attached to my own identities and memories; what is the good of being re-incarnated into a different person with no memory of my past lives? Then there's the idea of the void, the emptiness, the "oneness." Again, I'm attached to being this particular someone, so being nothing is not appealing. I have work to do on this issue.

In *The Second Half of Life,* Angeles Arrien uses the symbol of the threshold or gate for life transitions, but I think the beach offers an even more powerful symbol for me—it is the threshold between the familiar and safe land and the deep, mysterious, unknowable ocean, the stew from which we arose as humans and to which we ultimately return. It symbolizes death and birth.

Waves also have distinct phases, or a cycle of life, if you will. Waves can be created by wind, by changes in atmospheric pressure, by seismic events like earthquakes, explosions or landslides, or by friction. A wind-driven wave starts life as wind passes over still water. The air molecules break the surface of the water and furrow it, raising small ripples or tiny waves called "cat's paws." These ripples catch more of the wind's energy and grow into "chop" which can easily assume a chaotic, irregular pattern called a "sea," or with a gentle blowing wind, ripen into a wave. The wave can grow very large, depending on the distance it can run without encountering an obstacle, a concept called "fetch." When the wind dies down, the wave loses its peak and becomes a long, rounded, low swell. Swell can move for thousands of miles until it approaches a shoreline and turns into a breaker that crests and falls. If the breaker encounters a sandy beach, the swell rises and falls in regular waves. If the breaker encounters cliffs or rocky shore, it meets land in a violent encounter that tosses boulders into the air, throws the spray dozens or even hundreds of feet into the air, and forces air and water into rock fissures and fault lines, eventually eroding them.

So, too, our cycles of life have rhythmic and unpredictable waves. Some human lives are short and tempestuous; others follow the long rolling swell of years before cresting and dying on a sandy shore. We may not have much control over the elements—the wind, climate, seismic events of our lives, but sometimes we have a choice as to where and how our waves land. We can rail against the obstacles, tossing the boulders into the air or against unyielding granite cliffs, or we can choose to land with grace and dignity on the sandy beach. I'd like to think of my life ending as one long plunging breaker landing on a long sandy beach, flowing gently back into the deep blue sea and merging with all of life in the ocean. Perhaps I'll end up as a bright yellow chip stuck in a crack in the gray basalt stone that will delight some beach walker, or I'll be a smooth weathered ochre stone that someone carries in their pocket for comfort. Somehow, I'll end up on a beach.

The Beach as Threshold to Wisdom

"In every curving beach, in every grain of sand, there is the story of the earth." (Rachel Carson)

Thresholds are a symbol of change. Once crossed, we are never the same again. The pounding waves can literally "thresh" our souls, separating out the false chaff from the true essence, and leaving behind the deeper wisdom. The four major transition points or developmental tasks of elderhood that Angeles Arrien (*Second Half of Life*) identified as key for developing wisdom include the following paradigm shifts.

Moving from ambition to meaning (or from ego to spirit). With age, we shift from valuing what brings us status or material goods to what brings us meaning and purpose in life. When I moved, I sold all of my "valuables" and took only photographs of friends and families, and a few trinkets that reflected some deep connections with people or places. After all the material down-sizing, I was ready to start shedding ego. The ocean helps in this process, as it washes away all the extraneous stuff, leaving only the deep meanings. Similarly, I changed the way that I approached friendships, from seeking out people with external status, or who could help me "get" something I wanted, to seeking out personally meaningful relationships—friends that feed my soul, not my ego. Of course, this is an ongoing process and I have periods when ambition and ego swell to the size of a surfer's dream wave. But now I can feel the shift away from ego pulling me back constantly, the growing wisdom like an anchor keeping me from drifting back to my old ways.

Integrating processes of descent and ascent. Descent refers to going deeper into the darkness, the unknown, or our own shadow sides full of unresolved issues; and ascent reflects a greater awareness and authenticity outside of our selves. In beach metaphors, descent is the exploration of the ocean depths and all the scary things below the surface. Those scary things can continue to lurk just barely submerged, like icebergs, and affect our passage through life until we find the courage to look at them directly. For me, some of those scary underwater issues are fears of mortality and examining my conflict avoidance and pridefulness. Ascent is learning to ride the waves, confident and triumphant. Ascent involves transcending the fears and expectations, and learning to feel a part of the larger cosmos. When I deal with and transcend my fears, I can make my gifts and talents available to others, and become actively engaged in improving the world. But I guess I'm like most people, hoping to transcend and ascend to some glorious new future without doing the painful work of descent into the darkness of the shadow. I recognize the necessity of this work and realize how rewarding it can be to directly confront the shadow.

Integration of the external and the internal processes. The external includes what is seen and observed, such as memories and specific events of our lives. The internal is what is sensed, such as insights, dreams (especially the recurrent ones), and transcendent experiences. The integration of our internal and external experiences only comes about when we take time for reflection. A walk on the beach can take those external events, such as memories, and integrate them with our dreams and insights in ways that we did not connect before.

Waves are an interesting blend of external and internal. External forces like wind, earthquakes, or volcano eruptions start the energy flow that creates the wave, but the water molecules roll in a circle, so that internally, the water is stable. It is only the external energy that actually moves, made visible by the rising and falling of water. Similarly, the ocean is both an external place that we can visit, and an internal stew of salt and minerals inside our own bodies. Inside and outside, external and internal are merely socially constructed boundaries and are not "real." Integration work is about breaking down those boundaries and seeing the fluid interconnections.

Moving beyond polarity and duality to integration. This paradigm shift involves having tolerance for ambiguity and adopting both/and thinking. Rarely is anything either/or in real life—it is only our minds that try to create that certainty. Tides are only high or low for a split millisecond. Most of the time the tide is in some state of transition: it is going out or coming in. And the earth, sea, and sky are interconnected parts of a whole system, not separate entities. I think this dualistic thinking underlies much of my tendency to judge. I observe a behavior or hear a phrase, and judge it as good or bad. If I suspended judgment for a time and really listened, I'd see the gray areas. Tolerance for ambiguity and transitions allows us to experience the present moment rather than spend most of our time obsessing about a past event or anticipating some future trauma. Speaking just for myself, giving up the obsession with the past or future would give me much more time to spend on a beach somewhere!

Being a mentor or steward

"Educating people to understand, to love, and to protect the water systems of the planet, marine and fresh water, for the wellbeing of future generations." (Mission statement of the Cousteau Society)

Another key transition of the second half of life is becoming a mentor or steward. I have seen this manifest in several ways in my life. First I have witnessed a shift in my professional life away from a focus on my own individual academic projects, aimed at bringing promotion and personal advancement, to being more interested in mentoring others, and doing projects that promote social justice rather than individual gain. I have a deeper commitment to develop my spiritual self so that I can be a better role model and mentor (and a better friend, daughter, sister, partner, neighbor, and so on). Instead of viewing students as an obstacle to getting my own work done, as I was encouraged to do at my first academic job, I have a genuine interest in helping them manifest their own projects, and develop as scholars and community leaders. The process of mentoring others seems to be a spiritual calling, and my way of expressing generativity.

In another way, my hours spent on beaches and reading about the ocean has led me to figure out ways to be a better partner of the earth and seas. I feel compelled to learn as much as possible about saving the seas, which is really about the survival of the whole planet and everything on it, and putting this knowledge into practice in my everyday life. Being a steward of the seas means learning responsible use of the earth's resources. As I take breath, I remind myself that 70% of the oxygen I take in comes from the ocean, the other 30% from the plants on the land that rely on water from the ocean to survive. What am I doing that inhibits this oxygen flow? As I wash dishes or brush my teeth, I am mindful that water is a precious commodity, not to be wasted. When I eat, I think of the 16% of protein in my diet that comes from the ocean, where 70% of the commercial fisheries are now depleted (facts from David Helvarg, *The Blue Frontier*). I know I must look beyond those small individual efforts that I can take, and also join in collective efforts to change government policies and corporate activities that are destroying our outer home. Many years ago, Rachel Carson wrote a letter to the Washington Post that read in part:

> *"For many years public-spirited citizens throughout the country have been working for the conservation of natural resources, realizing their vital importance to the Nation. Apparently their hard won progress is to be wiped out, as a politically-minded Administration returns us to the dark ages of unrestrained exploitation and destruction. It is one of the ironies of our time that, while concentrating on the defense of our country against enemies from without, we should be so heedless of those who would destroy it from within."* (quoted in Matthiessen, Courage for the Earth, p. 44)

How true that statement still is today, as so much of our financial and human resources are put to war abroad and homeland security locally. These efforts do not make our future more secure. Becoming a steward of the beach starts with knowledge, but does not end there. It must move to direct actions on both the individual and collective levels. I yearn for the day when Homeland Security means a global effort to protect the earth and seas. The Blue Ocean Institute proposes that we develop a "Sea Ethic," noting that *"how the ocean is faring reflects how humanity is faring. In extending our collective sense of community beyond humanity and below the high tide line, we call for a Sea Ethic."* Amen.

Going Deeper
1. Reflect back on each decade of your life so far, and record the main lessons you learned. Look for patterns or themes, and practice looking for lessons learned rather than merely remembering stories. Where have you not taken action on life lessons and repeated old habits from the past?
2. Think about your relationship to transitions and uncertainty. How have you dealt with closure and moving on?
3. Where in your life have you seen the development of wisdom? In what ways are you wiser now than you were ten years ago? What fosters wisdom for you?
4. Where can you be a better mentor or steward in your life?

11
Change

"The face of the sea is always changing. Crossed by colors, lights, and moving shadows, sparkling in the sun, mysterious in the twilight, its aspects and its moods vary hour by hour."
(Rachel Carson, The Sea Around Us)

  The beach is never the same from one moment to another. The sand shifts with the tides and the winds, new delights wash ashore every minute, the color of the waves varies with the sunlight and seasons—deep blue in a warm summer sun, aqua after a rain storm, steely gray in the winter overcast, sea-green in a light fog. The breakers are foamy white or frothy gray, and the waves flow to the shore as long rolling swell or the sea has chaotic white caps as far as the eye can see. From sunrise to sunset, change is ever present; change is the nature of the beach. Change is the nature of our daily lives, as well, if only we pay attention. How often we create the illusion of sameness in our lives rather than appreciate the uniqueness of each moment. Recently, a friend said to me, "I wish I could hear the ocean at night. That monotonous sound would help me sleep." Her statement reminded me of a passage from Henry Beston's book, *The Outermost House*, where he expressed quite a different opinion about the sound of the ocean.

> *"The three great elemental sounds in nature are the sound of the rain, the sound of wind in a primeval wood, and the sound of outer ocean on a beach. I have heard them all, and of the three elemental voices, that of the ocean is the most awesome, beautiful, and varied. For it is a mistake to talk of the monotone of ocean or of the monotonous nature of its sound. The sea has many voices. Listen to the surf, really lend it your ear and you will hear in it a world of sounds: hollow boomings and heavy roarings, great watery tumblings and trampling, long hissing seethes, sharp, rifle-shot reports, splashes, whispers, the grinding undertone of stones, and sometimes vocal sounds that might be the half-heard talk of people in the sea. And not only is the great sound varied in the manner of its making, it is also constantly changing its tempo, its pitch, its accent, and its rhythm, now almost placid, now furious, now grave and solemn-slow, now a simple measure, now a rhythm monstrous with a sense of purpose and elemental will. (p. 43-44)*

It only takes a change of perspective to hear the incredible variations of sound in the sea. In fact, most of what we call change involves a shift in perspective. If we pay attention (wake up) and really listen to the world around us, monotony turns into vast variety and nuance. The world is characterized by change and variety, not constancy, yet we are often so resistant to the change.

I think of change as coming in two forms: the kind that is thrust upon us, unwanted, and that we resist (futilely), and the kind that we seek out--the transformative changes to improve the quality of our lives.

Unwanted Change

"We leap at the flow of the tide and resist its ebb. We are afraid it will never return." (Anne Morrow Lindbergh, Gift from the Sea, p. 108)

One week in mid January, we had a "weather" week. Storms blew in from the sea everyday with torrential downpours, high winds, hail, and occasional thunder and lightning. It was the kind of weather that made any travel difficult. Roads were flooded, visibility was poor, and wind instantly turned umbrellas inside out and useless. The storm came during my winter break, so I did not need to go to work, so for several days, I stayed indoors in my flannel pjs, watching anxiously out the window for a break in the weather. Five days passed without a beach walk, but on the sixth day, the sun shone again, so I headed for a familiar spot on the beach nearest to my house, San Francisco's Ocean Beach.

I parked at Taraval, crossed the road, and immediately noted the dramatic change in the landscape of the beach. There was a deep gully in the sand running from Great Highway to the beach. As I rounded the dune and headed down toward the water, there was a cement stoop with six steps descending down to the lower beach. Apparently the sand usually covers this stoop and the steps completely, because I had never seen them in my nearly five years of entering the beach at this spot. I turned to my right to walk north along the beach. The beach was stripped of sand at this point, and a gritty black tarry substance covered the land. The mile or two of low rounded dunes had been eroded, the seaward half of the dune scooped out by the high surf and wind of the past week, so that they resembled sandy cliffs instead of rounded dunes. The ice plant that had covered that side of the dune was strewn all over the beach, along with kelp, driftwood, and debris of all sorts. I was saddened and appalled by the sheer volume of the man-made litter—the plastic caps from soft drink bottles, the potato chip wrappers, and all the other garbage that the ocean had vomited up on the shore. I hoped that the detox had given some measure of healing to the sea, but I feared that the next high tide would merely sweep all the debris back out to sea.

This reflection about human litter and destroying the beautiful natural home we live on was becoming overwhelming, so I lifted my eyes from the shoreline and focused my sight on the edge of the water. The wind was still blowing at a fairly stiff pace, so the sea foam floated on the edge of the water, and blew across the beach in stiff peaks like a bubbly meringue. The waves were still choppy and chaotic, no long rolling and spilling over of waves as is typical of calmer days. I looked up. The sky above me was blue and clear, the moon just past the crescent phase shining above, and clouds rimmed the horizon in every direction. I was in the bowl of sunshine, on this unfamiliar terrain within the familiar landmarks of ocean to the west, mountains to the north and south, Twin Peaks and the Sutro Tower to the east.

The experience of this complete alteration of my familiar terrain had me shaken and upset for days. But it got me thinking a lot about my reaction to the changes and the lessons I could learn. Periods of storm and change are inevitable. I can dream of a life of peace and quiet and continuity, but in reality, life alternates between turmoil and peace, ease and striving, toxicity and healing. I can learn to hunker down during the worst of the storm, donning my psychic flannel pjs to wait it out patiently, knowing that the purging will be good in the end. The plants need to be uprooted and rearranged now and then; the beach needs a good cleansing and reshaping. Change is good, I tell myself, yet I resist change, and sometimes I passionately hate change.

I did not want my father to die. None of us did. Family and friends spent the first months after his diagnosis plotting how he could "beat this thing," and how we would manage his illness. It was hard to believe that he was sick, because he had been so robust and healthy up to the age of 69. We talked about his illness, but not his dying. I think we feared uttering the thought aloud, as if the words might make it come true sooner rather than later. Naming it would make it too real. I continued to deny or ignore all the signs of his dying as he turned into a frail old man in a matter of a few months. Nothing any of us could do could stop his physical dying process, but I wonder if we could have been more supportive of his internal letting go processes if we had listened to his wishes more closely.

Sometimes we think that change will not occur if we ignore all the signs, but nothing is more certain in life than change. As the old saying goes, nothing is certain in life but death and taxes. I did not want my mother to die either, but this time, I did not try to manage the situation as much, and I listened to her wishes and generally followed them, even when I did not like them. Every announcement of impending death or of losses to accidents has evoked some degree of resistance or denial. Not this person, not at this time. But for years, I was able to avoid thinking of my own mortality for more than a few anxious seconds before I pushed the thought away.

I did not want to age either. Selfishly, I wanted to gain wisdom and insight, and channel it through a young and healthy body. Menopause was not the traumatic event for me that it is for some women who are more vested in their identities as mothers, but I reacted to other aspects of aging more intensely, especially to the loss of energy and physical strength. But alas, I could not avoid the changes in my own body anymore than I could avert my parents' deaths. How do we learn to accept these unwanted, but natural changes with grace and dignity? Anne Morrow Lindbergh looked to the beach for answers:

> *"How can one learn to live through the ebb-tides of one's existence? How can one learn to take the trough of the wave? It is easier to understand here on the beach, where the breathlessly still ebb-tides reveal another life below the level which mortals usually reach…so beautiful is the still hour of the sea's withdrawal, as beautiful as the sea's return when the encroaching waves pound up the beach, pressing to reach those dark rumpled chains of seaweed which mark the last high tide." (Gift from the Sea, p. 109-110)*

Every new tide, every storm, and every change in life opens up another phase of our lives, provides us with new learning and new possibilities, and strengthens our own journey through life. Change pushes us along the road to maturity whether we are ready or not. I certainly learned lessons about death from my father's passing—I observed how he accepted his illness with grace and dignity, and how he died in peace. His dying was much like his living; quiet, humble, and dignified. I noted the impact he had on other people's lives as they came together to celebrate his life and support my family. I realized that I had a role model in stewardship in my father.

My ebb-tide was the burn-out and loss of meaning in life that followed his death, coupled with my growing dissatisfaction with my relationship and my job. I thought that I needed a totally different career, but discovered after a few years of searching that I needed a mental, physical, and spiritual change in perspective. I was in the right career, just not the right job placement. A year away from teaching gave me more time to reflect about what I liked and didn't like about my job and "course-correct" the issues that had lead to burnout. I returned to the classroom with a beachwise philosophy to support me. In other aspects of my life, I changed the external circumstances. I wanted (needed) to live by the ocean, somewhere where I could spent time out-of-doors year round. My mother often told me stories of my childhood love of being outdoors. She related that she would have to drag me indoors kicking and screaming at night, and then lock the doors to prevent me from escaping outside again. Moving to California allowed me to resume my childhood passion for the outdoors. I found as much delight in the nearby urban parks and beaches as the more removed wilderness where I could have solitude and silence within one hour's drive of a vibrant city. By slowing down and returning to nature's rhythm, I could make changes in my external circumstances that facilitated the internal changes related to my physical aging, and enhanced my personal growth and development.

Transformative Change

> *"It seems suddenly crucial to stay here and see the exact moment this tide turns. It should be easy; I know tidal charts are marked in minutes: high tide, say at 11:43 or 4:16. Even without a watch, isn't that an observable moment? The water will approach and approach and then, as if some lever pulled, some click that reverses the direction, the water will halt, begin to recede. I'll know it will*

come up no further. I'll be able to mark the line of high water with a stick, do what I've never been able to do in my life—say, here, this is the turning point." (Barbara Hurd, *Walking the Wrack Line, p. 26*)

My burnout and losses of important people in my life were unwanted changes, but they led to the second kind of change. That is the type of change that I desperately wanted, a change in the fiber of my being that would improve the quality of life and bring meaning and purpose into every moment. Like Barbara Hurd, I wanted an observable change, I wanted to be able to distinguish the turning point and say "this is when I changed." In reality, usually one can only identify the turning points in retrospect, after reflection and integration of those experiences. Change is a process, after all, not a discrete event. It's much more complicated than an event at one moment in time. That is, the event may be sudden—someone dies instantly in a car accident, an earthquake or fire destroys one's home. But the response to it takes a long time. There is an initial stage of shock, denial, grief, but over time, the experience can be integrated and lead to profound changes in perspective and/or behavior.

When I started meditating a few years ago, I yearned for a peak experience. I envied those who said that meditation brought them a deep sense of peace, harmony, ecstasy, bliss, or unity. But I was so thoroughly socialized in a Midwest stoicism that directed me to carefully control my emotions and stay in the middle, between the extremes of emotions, that I could feel little during meditation sessions. I also have a tendency to be in my head. People who know me well will be laughing now at this understatement. I've spent the past several years trying to spend more time in unexplored regions and give my head a vacation. Meditating on a cushion in the house was not the right format for me to open up my deeper self. I found it an excuse to delve into deeper thinking. It took meditative walking on a beach to begin to get me out of my head. As I opened up, I could see that transformative change could be a choice. I did not have to wait for a peak experience to descend unexpectedly. I could actually set up the conditions that would make me ripe for change.

Marilyn Schlitz, Cassandra Vietan, and Tina Amorok, in *Living Deeply*, summarized their decade-long study of transformative change and outlined the conditions that seemed to facilitate it. They surveyed over 9000 individuals who had experienced transformative life changes, like my "aha" moment on Ocean Beach. They also interviewed 50 wisdom teachers who help people facilitate these changes. First, they had to define what they meant by transformative change. Wisdom teacher Frances Vaughn offered this definition.

> *"transformation really means a change in the way you see the world—and a shift in how you see yourself. It's not simply a change in your point of view, but rather a whole different perception of what's possible (p. 19)…There's both an inner and outer dimension to it. It requires inner work and an appreciation for how that connects to being in the world and the outer work of action and service…the voyage of discovery lies not in seeking new vistas, but in having new eyes." (p. 20)*

Schiltz and her colleagues identified seven doors to transformation, or motivating forces that seemed to prompt or initiate the change process, showing that there is wide diversity in how people view the underlying "cause" of their life changes. These seven portals (or thresholds) to change are:

1. Pain (suffering, crisis, loss, hitting bottom);
2. Noetic experience (direct sensory or inner experiences that create subjective knowledge that can be pleasant or unpleasant, sudden or gradual, and result in awe, inspiration, wonder, revelation, or transcendence);
3. Non-ordinary states of consciousness (these can be plant-induced, or stem from breathwork, meditation, hypnosis, being in nature, rituals, or can be spontaneous);
4. Psychedelics (drugs used as a therapeutic tool, often under the supervision of a teacher; this does not include recreational drug use);
5. The influence of a profound teacher;
6. Finding the extraordinary in the ordinary (these experiences stem from activities such as reading an inspiring book, tending a garden, being introduced to new ideas, being in nature, a glance, sports or physical activities);
7. Time in nature.

Notice that time in nature is mentioned as part of several of these doorways, as well as warranting mention by itself. Angeles Arrien declared *"the transformational crucible is the outer world. In many ways, the outer is really a mirror of what the person is doing internally."* (p. 57 in *Living Deeply*). Some of these external world motivators could be consciously selected to enhance the possibility of transformative change. Of course, most of us would not deliberately choose pain and suffering as a portal to wisdom, but the other gateways can be tapped at any time to enhance our growth and development.

Solitary time on a beach opened me to noetic experiences and a subtle alteration of consciousness, as well as finding the extraordinary in the ordinary. My obsession with rocks is an example of that—I have learned to see incredible beauty in the stones strewn along the beach, and the boulders and cliffs that mark the borders between beach and land. Everywhere I look on the beach, there is beauty and wisdom; in the waves, the sand, the plants, the rocks, the creatures, the air, the light. Everywhere.

All the wisdom teachers that Schlitz and colleagues interviewed agreed that having a daily practice will facilitate transformative change, and there appears to be four essentials of transformative practice, regardless of what form the practice takes. They promoted these four essentials whether the practice was meditation, prayer, beach walks, yoga, or any other spiritual practice. These four components of change are:

❖ Intention: the will to change.
❖ Attention: mindfulness, being awake, shifting perspective.
❖ Repetition: practicing regularly, typically on a daily basis.
❖ Guidance: a teacher helps keep the practice on track, and guides the student in ways that avoid deepening pathologies.

In regards to this idea of deepening pathologies, Ken Wilber has often lamented that some people focus on only one or a limited range of growth activities, rather than approaching development as multifaceted. So if a person with passive-aggressive tendencies spends four hours a day meditating, but does not work on interpersonal skills, that person may only deepen their own pathology. They might have the illusion of being more serene or centered, but in actuality, their passive-aggressive behaviors work against the development of wisdom and true serenity. This is where guidance from a skilled teacher can help—that teacher can identify the areas that a person needs to work on and guide them to growth activities in the areas where they most need help.

I found the four essentials of practice, along with Ken Wilber's model, to be a helpful framework for my transformative practice. I had found a powerful teacher/mentor, and I was going to the beach a lot for solitary reflection. If I went to the beach with a strong intention for change and used the time to reflect on what I was learning from my teacher, I would enhance my capacity for real change. That insight was what changed my perspective of the beach as a place for relaxation and recreation, to the beach as a wisdom teacher.

I have come to recognize that working on my own personal growth is only one part of the process of transformational change. If I do not work on interpersonal skills, and identify ways to improve my community and larger work for the betterment of society, I cannot change myself. I need to work on both my internal self and the external world. What's the point of becoming a more compassionate and authentic person if there is no earth, no sea left to sustain life?

Going Deeper
1. How have you dealt with unwanted change in your life? Has your perspective about change evolved as you mature?
2. What would you really like to change about your life? How can you use the information about transformative change to effect change?
3. Outline a daily practice that you currently do, or would like to try. What effects have this practice had on your life? What can you do to deepen the practice?

12
Grounding and Connecting at the Beach

"I like the way stone feels so solid. And even though I know its history and probable future, I like, for now, the pleasure of lifting a single one. When I touch it, I can say, with a certain degree of confidence, this is a stone. I can run my fingers over its edges, lick its contours. I can't do that with water, my mother's element. I can see it, swim in it, cup a handful. But it's not possible to touch the sea. It's too amorphous, too vast, and like too much thought of the formless spiritual, it finally numbs me, splatters my attention. At the edge of the ocean, it's the stones that now ground me."
(Barbara Hurd, Walking the Wrack Line, p. 27)

I have been drawn to rocks for a long time, feeling a sense of grounding and centeredness when holding one in my palm. I have always loved skipping stones over a placid lake surface, striving for 4, 5, or maybe even 6 skips before the rock disappears beneath the surface. For years I have carried rocks in my pocket and rubbed the stones to remind myself to ground when I feel stressed. In my younger adult years, I believed that I was living the Simon and Garfunkel song (*"I am a rock; I am an island. And a rock feels no pain and an island never cries"*), drawn to stones and isolated places to avoid being hurt by other people.

Now I have a deeper understanding of the attraction of the rocks. They are an ancient part of the earth, reminding me of the earth's beginnings. The stones I am most drawn to now are the ones weathered by the sea, their sharp edges smoothed. I particularly like stones with lines of contrasting color shot through the stone—green lines coursing through reddish orange stones; white bands through brown or black stone. These smooth stones have been aged over millions of years. Wild rugged mountains are tamed to gentle, soothing, smooth stones by millions of years of tumbling in the ocean. My first year in California, someone told me about a Native American belief of one of the California tribes. They sought out stones that had a line all the way through the stone; these were "completion stones" that would help the one carrying the stone to finish a task that needed doing. I collected dozens of such stones and carry them on days when I'm faced with deadlines, or when some old issue that I have not resolved rears its ugly head and torments me.

The stones remind me that I am connected to earth and sea. Our bodies are about 70% water molecules. Correspondingly, oceans cover about 70% of the earth's surface. Like the earth, we humans have a rocky (bony) infrastructure that erodes over time and is cushioned by the salty water in our bloodstreams, cells, and joints. I agree with Barbara Hurd's observation that begins this section that the sea is hard to touch, to grasp, but the stones at its edge are concrete and connect me to something solid and reassuring. We need both qualities in our lives—the solidity and stability of stone and the fluidity of water. Theodore Roszak, in *Person, Planet,* stated *"we were mothered out of the substance of this planet. Her elements, her periodicities, her gravitational embrace, her subtle vibrations still mingle in our nature, worked a billion years down into the textures of life and mind" (p. 54).*

This view of the earth and sea as parents is a powerful metaphor for me, and apparently for many others as well. Many cultures of the world have a mother or grandmother archetype that includes the sea or other component of nature. I feel protected by that parental love; one that is unconditional and always available. When I forget that love and connection, the rock in my pocket reminds me.

One day I came across a large stone on Rodeo Beach, on which someone had painted these words: "The lord is my rock." As I reflected on this, I realized that the opposite was true for me, "the rock is my lord." The rock is my crucifix, my prayer beads, my holy icon symbolizing the spiritual path that I have chosen which follows nature's path along the sandy or rocky shore.

Connection to the Outer World and Others

"...walking along the shore of the resounding sea, determined to get it into us. We wished to associate with the ocean until it lost the pond-like look it wears to a country man." (Henry David Thoreau, Writings of Henry David Thoreau)

This comment of Thoreau's made me reflect on why I am so drawn to Baker Beach, an urban beach that faces the Marin headlands rather than the open sea. Baker Beach is located west of the Golden Gate Bridge, and the bridge's immense presence fills the landscape to the east. Directly across from the beach one can view the Marin Headlands, green grassy hills with clusters of trees at the highest points, and a lighthouse extending out into the golden gate strait at the northwest corner of the view. To the west, there is a glimpse of wide open ocean, but hemmed in by cliffs that protrude to cover the southwestern view. These landmarks shelter the beach. In addition to its geography, Baker Beach has swell and waves that crest and fall in long unbroken lines, and very close to the shore. When the waves are large (5-6 feet), the spray splashes 15-20 feet in the air and the wave crashes with a resounding boom. The beauty and symmetry of the waves keeps attention focused to the water's edge. All of these elements combine to make it feel safer there—the ocean feels more "pond-like" thus not so vast and mysterious. The scope of it all is more manageable to my Midwestern-socialized brain. I can connect to the sea, without the terrifying implications of the endless horizon of ocean. I have thought a lot about this connection to the safer aspects of the sea, and how my attraction to the beach and to beach stones, has restored my connection to nature in general.

Recently, an acquaintance was showing a group of people a ring she had purchased at an antique fair. The ring had belonged to some minor celebrity over 50 years ago, and she was explaining that it was very expensive, but worth it because she felt its history and a connection to that celebrity every time she wore the ring. I remember thinking to myself that the rock in my pocket, that I had retrieved from the surf the day before, had cost me nothing and was billions of years old, carrying the history of all creation in it. As humans we often lose perspective and think that only the history within our own memory or our nearest ancestors is important. The beach can remind us of the antiquity of the world—the water in the ocean is all the water there ever was, recycled by evaporation and returning to the earth as rain in an ancient cycle. Why can't we transfer some of the reverence we feel for relatively recent human-made structures to deeper respect and care of our ancient treasures, the beaches? The earth is the oldest "antique" we have, but as a culture, we have valued the human-made castles and mansions more than the redwoods and rocky shores.

Some authors have suggested that we have lost our connection to nature, which can result in over-valuing culture and technology, along with many other devastating consequences. Much of this writing has focused on the effects on children of "nature deficit disorder" which some suggest leads to attention deficit disorder, obesity, and childhood depression. Richard Louv (*Lost Child in the Woods*) showed how many communities in the United States have passed laws and policies that have dramatically reduced the availability of wild spaces for children to explore. Issues like increasingly rigid park rules and restrictions, overdevelopment, and fear of litigation have resulted in an alienation from nature in many people in our urban locales. Free play in nature stirs the imagination in ways that TV, video games, and internet surfing cannot do. The next generation has so much more to overcome than my generation, which at least in rural America, still had access to wild spaces and lived outdoors as much as weather (and parents) permitted.

Childhood memories of nature experienced through the senses endure throughout our lifetimes. Rachel Carson (*The Sense of Wonder*) pointed out that *"the sense of smell, almost more than any other, has the power to recall memories and it is a pity we use it so little."* This passage evoked a sensory memory of the lilac bushes in the front yard of my childhood home, and the lily of the valley that grew along the shady north side of the house. To this day, those two flower scents are among my favorites and bring back happy memories. I wish all children could have an intimate relationship with nature—it may be the only thing that saves the earth and seas from human destruction.

Centering

"Words are like the wind and the waves…flow with whatever may happen and let your mind be free; stay centered." (Chuang Tzu)

Another way to think about grounding (returning to our ground, our nature) is centering, or finding what Angeles Arrien (*Indepth Yearlong*) calls, *"the formidable middle."* In surfing, the key is to find one's center of gravity—that place that keeps one centered on the board and riding on the crest of the wave instead of being pummeled by the breaking wave. Center of gravity, according to the dictionary, refers to the place at which gravity acts—or pulls us toward the ground or the point in the body where weight is evenly distributed. Because humans move, the center of gravity is not a static location, but constantly shifting. So centering means to stay vigilant and constantly correct our course to return to the center even as life events continually push us off course.

Finding that center means to reconnect with our inner nature. We have to find our own center of gravity. So often, we have spent so many years off-balance that we cannot even identify our "formidable middle." We have to reestablish a relationship between our inner and outer worlds to find our center. Going to the beach is not so much about connecting with nature, because in reality, we are already connected—it is about recognizing that separation from nature is an illusion, or a delusion, as some authors think. Mark Coleman (*Alive in the Wild*) stated

> *We drink water from the faucet without feeling as if we are connected to the rain, streams, and oceans. We naively pollute the atmosphere without consciously thinking that we'll have to breathe in that same air. We eat our lettuce bought from the local store without appreciation for sunlight, earth worms, and other life forms that make the lettuce possible. Alan Watts, a pioneering Zen teacher, has written about this lack of awareness of interconnection, calling it a 'serious hallucination.'* (p. 74)

That separation from the world around us, whether we think of it as hallucination, delusion, or split personality, prevents us from being whole. We need to bring our inner and outer houses together again. If we were to awaken enough to see it, there is so much in nature that helps us recognize interconnectedness. For example, cultivating our beachwise philosophy will necessarily bring us to reconnecting with the moon. The moon affects our moods and bodily rhythms and projects a sense of wonder and mystery. The moon is also the major influence on the tides, and some think it may have come from the earth originally.

> *"The next time you stand on a beach at night, watching the moon's bright path across the water, and conscious of the moon-drawn tides, remember that the moon itself may have been born of a great tidal wave of earthly substance, torn off into space…scientists speculate that the scar on the earth that is the Pacific Ocean is where the moon was." (Rachel Carson, The Sea Around Us)*

Since moving to the coast and spending so much time on beaches, that are so affected by tides, I have grown much more aware of lunar cycles. The beach walkers who are oblivious to such things always amaze me. Once I was walking on Rodeo Beach during a negative low tide. I got up at 6 am so that I could experience the wonder of those very low tides when I can walk the hidden beaches and touch the starfish clinging to rocks. A woman walking a dog approached me and said, "I come here all the time and I've never seen the waterline so low. Do you know why that is?" I explained that it was a negative low tide. She responded, "I was here yesterday afternoon and it wasn't like this." Then I explained that the tides changed every day and that there had been a full moon the night before which causes more extremes in the tide. She listened with great interest and asked me how I knew this. I was shocked that someone who came to the beach every day could not have noticed the changes in tide. But I should know better—not everyone is awake to the beauty of our surroundings.

Trees also offer a powerful lesson in grounding. Trees near the ocean display such resilience and noble character. They are truly warriors! They adapt to the wind and the salty air, planting their roots deeply and bending to allow wind to blow through them, not topple them. Deep roots allow for flexibility on the surface. Trees also represent another kind of threshold—that between earth and sky—and are another powerful source of wisdom teachings.

Reconnecting

"There is, one knows not what sweet mystery about this sea, whose gently awful stirrings seem to speak of some hidden soul underneath." (Herman Melville, Moby Dick)

As a culture, we have developed a long pattern of separation of nature from society, of human from other living beings, of mind from body, and of matter from spirit. A philosophy and science based on these dualities has alienated us from Nature in its largest sense and our own personal natures as well. Too often we have chosen culture over nature; the socially constructed consumer-oriented, technological world is given a higher value than the natural world, and nature is sacrificed for the production of culture. If we recognized the soul in the sea, we might value nature more than the soul-less materialism of so much of our dominant culture.

Tom Hayden, in *The Lost Gospel of the Earth*, described three perspectives toward the earth that are prevalent today.

- ❖ The Lords of the Universe: a worldview that proposes humankind has a god-given right to get maximum use from the earth's resources, and that we were given dominion over the earth and all its creatures. Some formal religions support this view, and much of the government policy and corporate activities of the western world operate from this worldview.
- ❖ The Stewards of Nature: a perspective that nature can be manipulated or engineered by technology. This utilitarian viewpoint suggests that we can eventually fix any problem that we create now through more technology (that uses more natural resources). In other words, we look for the fix in the same technologies that are destroying the earth and sea, creating a vicious cycle of destruction. These first two perspectives create what Hayden calls *"sustainable pollution,"* not conservation or healing of the earth.
- ❖ Kinship with Nature: a spiritual connection with the earth that leads to valuing all of its living beings and all of its natural resources. This viewpoint seeks to blend culture and nature, and to find ways to survive and thrive and do minimal harm to the earth.

Much of the problem stems from the simplistic idea that there is only culture or nature, and that they are opposites. Dualisms of any kind imply that there are clear boundaries between things. Dualisms puts boundaries between "us and them," "nature and culture," "men and women," "the U.S. and Mexico," and "gay and straight." In reality, all boundaries are human-made. In reality, culture and nature are not "either-or" but "both-and." We can create a culture of nature loving or examine the nature of culture—culture stems from nature as much as nature stems from culture. Culture refers to how we understand and interpret nature.

When we open to new paradigms, such as kinship with nature (which is really an ancient paradigm, but one that we need to re-discover), the boundaries dissolve and the true interconnectedness is apparent. We are not merely connected or not connected to nature, but rather our connection is constantly shifting. We have brief moments of feeling totally connected and one with nature, and other brief periods of feeling totally disconnected and alienated. Most of the time, we are somewhere in the middle, along a vast continuum between the extremes. The beach can teach us so much about false boundaries—where is the boundary between the earth and the sea? It is ever shifting as waves flow in and out, and tides cycle from high to low and back again. Any boundary between land and sea only exists as a mirage in our own heads. Our idea of duality between living and inanimate is also artificial. Who can spend time at the beach without feeling that the ocean is alive? That the rocks "thrill with life?" We carry the ocean with us every day in all of our cells, if we only pay attention. Awakening and paying attention facilitates our reconnection with the sea, with our ancient origins. Awakening will also foster the kinship with nature that we desperately need to survive as a species.

Going Deeper

1. Mark Coleman offered a water meditation (p. 110), which I've condensed here.

    Sit before, or imagine, a body of water. Consider that every cell in your body contains the same ingredients as that water, and contemplate your watery nature; your tears, blood, lymph, mucous, saliva, urine, and sweat. Give gratitude that these fluids cleanse and moisturize all the cells of your body, lubricate your joints so you can walk and move freely, and help you digest food and eliminate waste products from your body. Think of how water flows from that external body of water, enters your own unique body to nourish and cleanse, and then exits to reform with the streams, rivers, and oceans. All water has undergone countless cycles through all living creatures through-out all time. The water now in your body may have passed through a cypress tree, a squirrel, some poison oak, and a person on the other side of the world. Give thanks for the gift of the water of life, the water that connects us all on a very intimate level.

2. What helps you to stay grounded or centered? If you have a tendency to leave your body and retreat to the mind during stress, here are some suggestions for grounding activities:

    - Plant your feet firmly on the floor, focus on the stability, and the connection with the earth below you. Pay attention to the physical sensations that ground you through your feet.
    - Imagine a root extending from your body down into the ground, going deep enough to hold you steady, yet allowing you flexibility and movement above ground.
    - Carry a beach rock in your pocket; hold it in your hand in times of stress or need for focus.
    - Have a beach photo or poster in your office space.

13
Fear: Tsunamis, Sharks, Pain, and Other Terrors

"Alone in a field or at the seashore...we feel closer to the mystery of life and death...nature seems to want us to remember death." (James Hillman, Talking on the Water)

During the half century that I lived in the land-locked Midwest, I had one recurrent nightmare that regularly disturbed my sleep. I would awaken trembling, out-of-breath, and off-balance for the next few days. In the dream, a giant wave was bearing down on me, a nano-second from engulfing me. I always woke up just before the water closed over my head, and often wondered what would happen if the dream wave ever actually did overtake me. You might ask why would a person with a fear of enormous waves move to the ocean? Interestingly enough, since moving to within a stone's throw of the ocean, I have not had that dream. I don't know what to make of that. I am still afraid of the vastness and depths of the ocean. I have little desire to be on it or in it, except to walk in its wake, no desire to take a small boat off shore, no yen to snorkel, surf, or scuba dive. I can still remember my fascination tinged with terror when I read Thor Heyerdahl's books about his experiences traversing the ocean on a tiny raft or a bamboo boat, of his vivid descriptions of the vastness of the sea. The idea of the depths and immensity of the ocean still make my heart pound and my pulse race. I'm terrified of sharks to the point that I cannot watch those shark attack TV shows, and I fear the darkness of the deep water. It seems like the open sea epitomizes the unknown and triggers my primal fears. Do we carry the fears of our sea-ancestors who lived in an eat-or-be-eaten world in the murky depths? Some days it feels like my life has become constricted by all the fears that surface regularly from the depths of my murky psyche.

Rachel Carson (*The Sea Around Us*) noted that some natural phenomenon of the sea, like the maelstrom, a gigantic whirlpool, and tidal bores, which carry flood tides up the mouth of the river as a single huge wave, are real dangers. They have also become metaphors for the dangerous and scary things in our psyches. Edgar Allen Poe effectively used the maelstrom to induce terror in his readers, and countless stories use sea monsters to symbolize primal human fears. Godzilla rose from the sea to trample and destroy civilization; the Loch Ness monster lurks out of view to snatch the life from us. A curse and a blessing of human evolution is our ability to anticipate future events. The blessing is that we can anticipate dangers and prepare for them, the curse is that the anticipatory fear may blanket us like a dense fog and interfere with happiness and contentment.

I am drawn to the relative safety of the point of transition from land to sea. My safety zone is to explore the ocean at its very edge…the accessible places where the ocean is less intimidating and even inviting. The beach is a place of recreation and relaxation, where families frolic with their dogs, a place of tranquility and relative calm. Waves may crash near the beach, but the cresting and spilling over of waves seems somehow controlled at the beach, not wild and chaotic, like movies of storms at sea with gigantic waves washing over rocky prominences, rendering boats to kindling on the rocks or twenty foot tidal bores bearing down a river. I feel safe at the beach. This safety is an illusion, of course. Since I have lived here, the newspaper has recounted numerous deaths of individuals who were innocently strolling on the beach and were swept out by a sleeper wave, walking on a cliff that eroded and dropped them to the sea, or were caught in a rip current while swimming or surfing. Life is not without danger and fear is part of the normal life cycle.

Rip currents are a good metaphor for many dangerous but hidden life situations. Rip currents are created by waves breaking over sandbars, raising the water level between the shoreline and the sandbar, which in turn causes currents to run parallel to the shore. These parallel currents converge and rush back to the sea between breaks or channels in the sand bars, sucking swimmers out to sea. Any beach with breaking waves can have rip currents, and these currents can vary in width from a few feet to over 300 feet. They also vary in speed, from 1-2 feet per second to 8 feet per second. More than 100 people die in the U.S. each year after being swept up by a rip current, and rip currents account for 80% of lifeguard rescues. The key to escaping a rip current is to swim parallel to the shore until you reach the point where the current weakens and you can angle toward the shore.

This can be a powerful lesson for many life circumstances in which we find ourselves. Sometimes, external forces that are not of our own making catch us unawares. These forces are beyond our control. If we try to escape them directly, we may drown, but if we "go with the flow" calmly while we evaluate the situation, we may find the break in the current, or swim to the weaker point that will allow us to escape. Fear can keep us from having a cool head and pacing ourselves. When we give in to fear, we futilely struggle against a stronger force, causing more pain and suffering than if we face the fear and consider our options.

Fear of Death and Dying

"Do you think a leaf that falls to the ground is afraid of death? Do you think a bird lives in fear of dying? It meets death when death comes, but it is not concerned about death; it is much too occupied with living...It is we humans who are always concerned about death-because we are not living. That is the trouble; we are dying, we are not living." (J. Krishnamurti, All the Marvelous Earth, p. 52)

Much human anxiety stems from the fear of dying. Nature can show us the natural cycle of life and death as J. Krishnamurti pointed out. The fear of death is a big one, and it seems to me, rational. Death is the ultimate unknown, and it seems natural to fear what we do not understand. I have fears crop up all the time—fear of heights, fear of earthquakes, fear of my car plunging off a cliff when I drive on Highway 1, fear that I'll trip and fall when walking on some deserted trail and be stranded alone. In some of these cases, the fear might be useful. It reminds me to be prepared and to be careful because there are real dangers in the world. Other fears seem to have a less direct connection to reality. These are fears of events over which I have no control. Some of my other fears are exaggerated out of proportion to their actual risk.

I often fear that I'll die of the same disease that took my father. Many nights I have experienced panic attacks when muscle twitches and jerks keep me from sleeping. Ultimately, I will die of something, and have no choice about what that is. For six years, I feared that I might not have another intimate relationship after losing a soul-mate, and that I would age alone. Ultimately, I will age alone whether I have a partner or not, but I finally did get past the grief of losing a soul-mate, and I am in a very mature, loving relationship now. I believe that our emphasis on youth in this culture and the countless remedies and procedures to halt or reverse aging all stem from our fear of dying. Aging is the visible marker that we are creeping closer to death. What a paradox our culture presents us in regards to death and dying. On one hand, it is a taboo topic to discuss one's own death, yet TV and movies are full of images of violent death. Murder is a spectator sport in our culture, but we remove our dying relatives to hospitals, then morgues and closed coffins to keep death at bay.

The fear of death creates a fear of aging. I cannot leaf through a popular magazine without encountering hundreds of messages in the advertising and the articles that urge me to stave off aging—to get rid of my wrinkles, to keep my skin smoother and blemish-free ("ugly age spots!"), and to color my hair to remove any trace of gray. There is little advice about being a wise elder, but lots of information about retiring to a senior living center, out of the way of the younger people of the culture. This is an area that needs much stewardship in our culture. We who are entering our elder years must become those stewards, showing the youth of our world that aging is a beautiful and natural process. We admire the whitened bones of a piece of driftwood and the ancient polished stone—why do we devalue the signs of age in a human body? We must speak out about this injustice done in our culture to those who are aging, because we are missing out on so much wisdom that could enrich our lives.

All the Other Fears

"Break, break, break

On thy cold gray stones, oh sea."
(Alfred Lord Tennyson)

But what about all the irrational fears that human beings harbor? Why do we fear being our authentic selves, fear the disapproval of another person, or fear making fools of ourselves? These irrational fears constrict our lives. I'm full of them. I'm afraid to sing or dance in public because I might be embarrassed. But so what? What harm does a little embarrassment do to anyone? I am afraid to speak up in certain situations when I think others know much more than I do; I fear looking foolish. Is it because of my own judgmental nature? Do I judge others as foolish, and don't want to be seen that way myself? Yes, I have to admit that sometimes I do think someone is acting foolishly and feel embarrassed for that person. I know I am projecting my own fears on them. The work of refraining from judgment is a difficult one for me, and an issue I need to mull over many a day on a beach. And what about those fears of being vulnerable? Why do I fear being myself with certain people? Why would I want people to like me if I'm not being me?

On a second reading of this section, I decided to look up the origins of the word "embarrassment" and noted that the definition is feeling "self-conscious." As I reflected on that, I wondered when it became a bad thing to be self-conscious? Isn't that what we strive for in the journey toward enlightenment? Perhaps if we were all a bit more self-conscious in our interactions with other people, we would be better able to sort out our reactions. Am I feeling embarrassed because I revealed a bit of my shadow side? Am I embarrassed because I engaged in a comparison with another person, and now feel a little superior? If I know more of my motives for my behaviors and reactions, I can take responsibility for them.

On an intellectual level, and in the light of day, I can be rational about all of my fears. I know that dreading some possible future catastrophe, or minor embarrassment, prevents me from fully engaging in life in the present. It is exhausting to carry around these fears, and they keep me from living in the present moment. The beach is the place that best helps me stay present and get in touch with the inner peace and detachment from which to view these fears. I sometimes tell myself, when the fears about having a serious illness are threatening to move from vague anxiety to panic attack, if I am going to die in a year or two (or tomorrow) would I rather stay here at home and worry, or go to the beach? So I go to the beach whenever I am able. John Muir's description of his first earthquake illustrates one way that a person might experience an "awesome" event of nature and balance realistic fear with wonder:

> *"I was awakened by a tremendous earthquake, and though I had never before enjoyed a storm of this sort, the strange thrilling motion could not be mistaken, and I ran out of my cabin, both glad and frightened, shouting, 'A noble earthquake.'…All nature's wildness tells the same story—the shocks and outbursts of earthquakes, volcanoes, geysers, roaring, thundering waves and floods, the silent uprush of sap in plants, storms of every sort—each and all are the orderly beauty-making love-beats of nature's heart." (In Chris Highland, Meditations of John Muir, Nature's Temple, p. 41)*

What a great perspective—to be glad and frightened at the same time seems to be a reasonable response to our fears of the unknown. This is particularly good advice for us living in California, where the threat of the "big one" is always hanging over us. We constantly live on "shaky ground." Earthquakes are inevitable, like aging and death, and it's better to be prepared for those events than to ignore or repress our fears. The key is in balance—prepare but do not obsess. Respect, but do not fear nature's power. As Angeles Arrien says, *"There's my plan and the mystery's plan. Trust in the mystery, but have a back-up plan."*

I would like to shed those trivial fears—the ones about feeling silly, embarrassed, or foolish. It would do me good to act out some of the childlike wonder of the world by singing, dancing, and just being silly. I am taking small steps in that direction and asking for help when I go to the beach. I am practicing vulnerability by admitting my fears—not indulging them or dramatizing, but bringing my awareness to them and giving them a name. I am stepping out of my comfort zone to try new things. So far, none of my fears have been realized.

The immense, deep oceans have tremendous power to absorb our pains and fears without any negative consequences. When we are honest about our pain and fears with other people, we are sometimes hurt when we share highly personal information. Some people may exploit our vulnerability or use the information to hurt us. On the other hand, being vulnerable may also create greater intimacy and deeper communication. We may fear overburdening others with our irrational fears, driving them away because our terrors trigger their own fears. When we have pains or fears that we do not want to share with others for whatever reason, the ocean can take them. Think of the emotional storm that fear can create inside of us--the waves of emotion breaking violently on the shores of our consciousness, raising white caps of anxiety-- and cast them into the chaotic waves tossed on blustery winds of a storm at sea. See how small our own fears are when dumped into the billions of gallons of sea water that dilute them. Letting loose of those fears by casting them into the sea can be a way of healing. So often our fears are intensified because we repress, ignore, or deny them—they go underwater and bite our toes like little sharks or sting like jellyfish. To distract us from facing our fears, our ego defense system kicks in, but that takes a lot of energy. Being in nature can allow our defense systems to relax and put us in a better frame of mind and spirit to handle those fears. Mark Coleman (*Awake in the Wild*) referred to a research study that found showing people pictures of nature scenes after a stressful event helped them to reduce their stress and calm down in a matter of minutes. If just looking at a picture of a beach is calming, imagine what the real thing can do!

Going Deeper
1. What fears keep you from sleeping at night? Are they "rational"?
2. When you experience fear, try a beach imagery practice. Imagine yourself at a peaceful, sunny, warm beach, with gentle waves washing away the fears, cleansing you of doubts and worries. Better yet, if you can, go to the beach or other place in nature and collect sticks or rocks that symbolize your fear. Toss these items one by one into the ocean or bury them, asking for them to be taken from you.
3. Think of fear as a "prison" and imagine yourself acting out this poem from Rumi:

Become the sky, Take an axe to the prison wall
Escape, Walk out like someone suddenly born into color

What do you need to take the axe to?

14
Wonder, Inspiration, and Joy

"And then, the unspeakable purity - and freshness of the air! There was just enough heat to enhance the value of the breeze, and just enough wind to keep the whole sea in motion, to make the waves come bounding to the shore, foaming and sparkling, as if wild with glee." (Anne Bronte, from Agnes Grey)

The mystery of life is what creates our sense of wonder, joy, curiosity, and inspiration. Our existence and that of the earth and seas is miraculous, yet how often we allow our everyday routines and worries to numb us to the wonders of life. One fall afternoon, I had a very strange and disorienting experience. I was driving home from work on Great Highway, along the Pacific Ocean, a route I take almost every day. I know every inch of this stretch of coastline, or so I thought. It was overcast above—a high fog, but I could see that it was sunny across the bay in the Marin Headlands. I was gazing at the familiar view as I drove north, the tip of the Marin Headlands with the Point Bonita lighthouse a white dot in the distance, sticking out past the white box shape of the Cliff House restaurant on the San Francisco side. But to my shock and surprise, on the coastline north of Point Bonita, a spit of land with an exposed sandstone cliff rising from the ocean and a rugged hillside dotted with buildings, was shining in stark detail. I could see houses with front porches and chimneys on rooftops. It looked so close—as if the Golden Gate Strait had closed up and the land rejoined the San Francisco peninsula with the Marin headlands. I thought for a moment that I was hallucinating.

As soon as I was able, I pulled off the road into one of the beach parking lots and leaned on the sea wall, staring in disbelief. How many times had I walked this beach, or drove this stretch of highway and had never seen this point of the landscape. There was a cluster of houses nestled on the hillside—why had I never seen this before? Was it a town? I figured it must be above Muir Beach, but could not recall what the north side of that beach looked like—were there really that many houses there? I stood there for at least 20 minutes, absorbing this new view. The only explanation I could construct at the time was that the late afternoon sun was shining from the west at an angle that spotlighted this stretch of coastline that was usually in shadow. It was a unique combination of sun shining on the headlands, and high fog overhead that created this view. I left with a sense of wonder and awe that the familiar could be made so unfamiliar, and grateful that I was paying attention to the horizon as I drove, instead of being lost in thoughts about the day. Now, every day I glance in that direction, but I have not had a repeat performance of that particular view. Maybe it was a once in a lifetime event, and I was privileged to witness it. The experience reminded me to pay attention, because something new and wondrous could appear at any moment.

The opposite of wonder and joy is boredom. Angeles Arrien (*Second Half of Life*) shared that the written Chinese word for boredom consists of two characters: one meaning "heart" and one meaning "killing." Thus, boredom wounds the heart by closing us off to the wonder of life. It is pretty hard to feel bored at the beach—the challenge is to hold the wonder of the beach in our hearts throughout the rest of our days. It is important to examine the triggers of boredom, that deadening sensation that closes our hearts to the glorious experience of life.

Wonder

"For a while, as dark set in and the moon lit sea and mountains, it all opened out unto nameless color, shape, and movement. Softly, everything came alive. Yes, this is it. All of Existence together is alive." (Robert Kull, Solitude, p. 151)

Beachwise living is a practice of staying open to the wonders of life and to the inspiration and creativity that come with that sense of wonder and curiosity. We must resist the temptation to go back to sleep and instead stay awake to the beauty of nature and the surprises that constantly manifest. Living in San Francisco has opened my eyes anew to nature's beauty. I once felt this connection to the mystery, and now I have regained it. As a youth, I loved trees (and I still do). I can remember lying on the ground, looking up at the sky through the branches. I spent hours sitting six feet above the ground in the crook of a tree, talking to my childhood friend, Donna. I played in the leaves of trees every fall, and have a visceral memory of the crisp crackle and dry musky smell of the dried leaves as I tromped through them. In winter, snow or ice would coat the bare branches of deciduous trees, turning them into luminous sparkling sculptures. Every tree is unique and symbolizes connection and grounding. With deep roots anchoring the tree to the earth, it can extend its arms to the heavens without fear. It sways in the wind, flexible, yet firm. When my father was dying and I could not sleep, I often went to the sofa in the sunroom and sprawled out under a skylight to watch the night sky through the branches and leaves of an old ash tree that shaded my backyard. I drew comfort from the creaking and groaning of the branches in the wind and the ever-changing patterns of shadows that the leaves tossing in the wind created on the walls of my house. The tree was just budding when he was diagnosed, and was in full leaf when he died. "Let him live through another fall ablaze in tree color," I begged, but it was not to be.

Now I'm more inclined to focus on the dynamic wonder of the waves, the solid beauty of rocks and shells, the unpredictable joy of spotting a sea mammal, and the amazing textures of the sand and rocks. Gary Greenberg, in *A Grain of Sand*, photographs beach sand with a microscope. What is revealed is truly amazing. Sand that appears beige to the naked eye is actually a rainbow kaleidoscope of colors, sizes, shapes and textures. Sand is one of the later stages of matter that has evolved from the original lava landmass, eroded by the ocean currents, melting and grinding glaciers, rain, and floods. The rocks fall from mountains to become boulders in the river, ground to pebbles and then sand. Later it erodes further to mud, slit, and clay, which recomposes into soil and rock to begin another cycle. Sand also contains the remains of coral reefs and multitudes of sea creature's shells and bones. Unfortunately, beach sand increasingly includes beads of Styrofoam and plastic, substances that choke and kill birds and fish. Greenberg's photographs were stunning and eye opening, and I learned to see sand through new eyes.

The first year I lived in San Francisco, during our weekly phone conversations I would often tell my mother about visiting different beaches up and down the coast. On several occasions, she asked, puzzled, "Aren't all beaches more or less the same?" I thought a lot about that perception. In my experience as a dedicated beach bum, no two beaches are alike, and no single beach is the same from one day to the next. The sand varies by color, shape, texture, and composition, yet appears uniform to the naked eye. The same beach is different from one visit to another depending on season, time of day, and state of the tide. There may be a lesson about human diversity here. Even though we tend to blend in with our coworkers, family members, or neighbors at first glance, if you look more closely, we are all as unique as each grain of sand on the beach. The uniformity is an optical illusion, created when all the colors blend together. We need to be open to looking deeper and not relying on the surface appearances of people or things. Beneath the bland appearance of many of us human beings lay the unique shapes, textures, and colors that represent our quirky personalities and our gifts and talents.

Sand, often seen as the monotonous, dull part of the beach, holds many wonders to those who pay attention. Henry Beston (*The Outermost House*) had this to say about the sand on Cape Cod:

> *"It is no easy task to find a name or a phrase for the colour of Eastham sand. It's tone, moreover, varies with the hour and the seasons. One friend says yellow on its way to brown, another speaks of the colour of raw silk. Whatever colour images these hints may offer to a reader's mind, the colour of the sand here on a June day is as warm and rich a tone as one may find. Late in the afternoon, there descends upon the beach and the bordering sea a delicate overtone of faintest violet…there is always*

reserve and mystery, always something beyond, on earth and sea something which nature, honouring, conceals." (p. 13-14)

I did not truly recognize the wide diversity of the sand on my local beaches until I started taking pictures of rocks on the beach. When I printed the pictures, I saw that some beach sand was fine, with delicate lacey patterns. Other beaches consisted mostly of small pebbles, others larger cobbles or coarse sand. Some fine sand was dark and some light, almost white, in color. After some time, I was able to look at the sandy background of a photo of a rock, and know which beach it came from.

Another mystery of the beach is the singing sand. As Bosker and Lencek describe it,

"at many of the world's beaches, sands exhibit a remarkable musical gift. When the wind passes over them, sands can produce a variety of sounds from the silky rustling and dog-like barking on the dunes of Kauai, Hawaii, to the eerie whining of the sandstone cliffs on the Isle of Eigg in the Hebrides…No one really knows what produces these bizarre acoustic phenomena, although scientists have attributed them to everything from the mechanical friction of salt-coated sand grains to the percussive effect of tiny pockets of air released by shifting sand." (p. 50)

On most beaches, we must acclimate to the overwhelming sound of the ocean's background roar and the intermittent crashes of waves before we can hear the more subtle sounds. If we are open to them, the wondrous sounds of singing sand, bird calls, the wind rustling the dune grasses, and whispering sand awaits us.

I also found a renewed sense of wonder in the rocks on the beach. So often, particularly at low tide, rocks of every size, shape, color, and texture litter the beach. The waves create a satisfying rustling, tumbling rock sound as they pass over the rocks. I stroll, head down, engrossed in the spectacle. I lose track of time, do not notice other people, dogs, surfers, or anything but the glory of the rocks. Each beach walk is like a treasure hunt, or a stroll through an art gallery.

Another part of the wonder of the oceans is the sense of being interconnected with all things. We breathe in air, extract oxygen that gives us life, exhale carbon dioxide that plants need to live and the plants in turn produce food and oxygen for us. All the plant, animal, and human remains after death end up back in the ocean from whence we came. Understanding ecology, the science of the interconnectedness is vital for our survival, but also miraculous in and of itself. As Ernest Callenbach noted (*Ecology*):

"ecological knowledge brings us face-to-face with the underlying paradox of our place on Earth today; understanding the marvelous intricacy, variety, and beauty of life gives us endless delight, but coupled with this joy comes the pain of seeing how grievously destructive to the web of life are our industrial, agricultural and personal activities as we now practice them." (p. 2)

Again, there is a lesson about human diversity and interconnectedness in the lessons of ecology. We can have endless delight in the beauty and variety of human life, yet also experience the pain of war and conflict between people who do not celebrate their differences, but try to impose their beliefs and practices on others. In the long run, we are on this earth together and must find ways to live harmoniously with each other and with our world.

Inspiration

"In modern times, both the automobile and the airplane were launched on beaches. The Wright brothers made their first flights at Kitty Hawk, in the Outer Banks of North Carolina. Farther south, at Daytona Beach, Florida, early automobile models were tested on 18 miles of hard-packed sand that would continue to be used as a stock car race track until 1959. Just a few miles south of Daytona, on the beach of Cape Canaveral, the first manned flights into space proved once again that the beach has always marked the threshold of human experience." (Bosker & Lencek, Beaches, p. 85)

Throughout history, there have been countless examples of how individuals have been inspired by or at the beach. Not only has the beach been the birthplace of the transportation industry, it has spawned creative ideas and powerful fiction and nonfiction works, as well as transformed the lives of individuals. This is not to imply that merely sitting on the beach will miraculously produce great ideas or launch new careers (although sometimes it does!), because most of the time, we have to work at it. The ideas are only so much flotsam unless we take action, and sometimes we avoid taking action because it seems like too much work. This passage from Mary Parker Buckle's book (*Margins*) struck me as highly appropriate in my musings on inspiration.

"Wildlife research is glamorous stuff to read about in an armchair where such realities as heat, biting insects, grime, improvised food, and disappointment—the constant disappointment of missed opportunities and simple judgment—do not intrude on the cooly worded summaries. Nor do wildlife reports provide many clues to the years of grueling effort that sometimes go into a single insight." (from George Reiger, Wanderer on My Native Shore, in Buckles, p. 266)

Isn't this also true of acquiring wisdom? If we gain our knowledge through books, TV, movies, and the condensed stories of other people, those sources generally leave out the drudgery, tedium, missteps, and other details. Actual beachwise wisdom is not attained merely by sitting on pristine sand dunes on sunny warm days. Sunbathing usually isn't enough, and it's not always easy. Sometimes the wind blows sand in our faces and eyes, or the waves are so large that they block passage from one part of a beach to another. Some days the sand fleas bite and the sun burns. Wisdom comes from the accumulation of life experiences: the good, the bad and the ugly; the easy, hard, and the in-betweens; in sickness and health; good weather and torrential downpours; through egos battered and bruised; high and low tides; sun and fog; and through feelings hurt and hearts broken. To "inspire" is to draw breath—all is wondrous whether we experience the event as positive or negative at the time. Sometimes the biting flies wake us up and force us to attention; sometimes the fog may mirror our internal confusion and remind us to pay attention to the fog horns in life that provide guidance lest we dash our hopes on a rocky prominence. All of life's experiences are grist for the mill of wisdom. Walking meditation on the beach may be a tool for problem-solving, but the solutions generated must be put into action.

Joy

"As you walked on the beach, the waves were enormous and they were breaking with magnificent curve and force. You walked against the wind, and suddenly you felt there was nothing between you and the sky, and this openness was heaven. To be completely open, vulnerable…To the hills, to the sea, and to man—is the very essence of meditation. To have no resistance, to have no barriers inwardly toward anything, to be really free, completely from all the minor urges, compulsions, and demands with their little conflicts and hypocrisies, is to walk in life with open arms. And that evening, walking there on that wet sand, with the sea gulls around you, you felt the extraordinary sense of open freedom and the great beauty of love which was not in you or outside you—but everywhere." (J Krishnamuri, All the Marvelous Earth, p. 67)

Joy is another of those elusive concepts. We know it when we experience it, but the sensation is hard to put into words. It is on a continuum ranging from contentment to bliss, encompassing a wide variety of quite different sensations. In some Buddhist writing, joy is described as freedom from suffering. In some other writings, joy is described as ecstasy. For example, Rumi once said, *"I know I'm drunk when I start this ocean talk,"* suggesting that he lapsed into giddy prose when speaking of the sea. Spending time on the beach can enhance all types of joy. In the most everyday sense, we tend to think of the beach as a place for vacation, with the joy of being free to choose how to spend our time.

"With their love of the sea, the Romans invented the beach holiday. Passionate bathers, they constructed luxurious coastal retreats, public natatoria, and leisure outposts where both the elite and commoners escaped from the heat and bustle of urban life. Rome's finest thinkers, writers, and statesman…took frequent seaside vacations, which they structured on the formula of otium cum dignitatae, relaxation with dignity. These early prototypes of the working holiday involved a finely balanced regime of meditation, physical exercise, intellectual stimulation, and sensual pleasure." (Bosker & Lencek, Beaches, p. 71)

I love that phrase "relaxation with dignity" but I also believe that letting one's hair down and getting silly on the beach is always a fun option. Who doesn't feel a child-like joy on the beach? The most cynical of teenagers, the most serious of adults can delight in the flying of a kite, the frolicking of dogs in the surf, and the laughter of children playing in the surf or digging in the sand. The beach is often associated with vacation, with rest and rejuvenation. That joy of human and nature connection and shared recreation is one of the great attractions of the beach. There is no doubt that the beach inspires happiness.

Mark Coleman (*Awake in the Wild*), distinguished between blissful experiences, which tend to be fleeting and transient, and a deep, more lasting sense of meditative joy that comes from awakening. He noted that *"spiritual joy is a quieter, internal process we carry with us, like an inner light and inner smile"* (p. 167-8). Perhaps that is what the Romans meant by relaxation with dignity. The secret is to find ways to carry spiritual joy into all of my everyday activities, so that inner smile sustains me through the too-long meeting, the traffic jam, and the other trying moments of the day. I aspire to capture the inner light that blazes in me on the beach, and let it glow in all parts of my life. I do this by carrying a beach rock in my pocket, by having a beach scene as my screen saver at work, and using beach visual imagery throughout the day to relax and recapture my inner beach bum smile.

Going Deeper
1. Where in your life have you experienced that deep sense of joy that seems to come from the innermost part of your being? What situations foster that kind of joy?
2. What inspires you? Are you living out your aspirations in your work, your relationships, your community, or your creative endeavors? If not, how can you bring inspiration into your daily life?
3. What does joy feel like to you? Are you happy with where you are in terms of experiences of joy?
4. How can you bring more wonder, more joy into your life?

15
Protection, Resources, and Healing

*"Late, by myself, in the boat of myself,
no light and no land anywhere,
cloud cover thick. I try to stay
just above the surface, yet I'm already under
and living within the ocean." (Rumi)*

The shoreline can be a perilous place with sneaker waves, riptides, tsunamis, jellyfish, sudden squalls, and fog, but it is also a place of healing and joy. The secret is to engage all the protections available to us to minimize the dangers, so that we can trust in the healing power of nature. Sometimes trusting in nature and living under and within the ocean is just what we need. We have so many gifts and talents that help us to survive and thrive in the world, but sometimes recognizing and using those gifts and talents can be a challenge. So much in our culture causes us to doubt or repress the many resources we have access to within ourselves. But if we stop to think about it, most of us have both internal and external protections and resources that we can draw upon in times of need. The beach contains many metaphors of protection.

Protection

"Metaphysics is a dark ocean without shores or lighthouses, strewn with many a philosophic wreck." (Immanual Kant)

Protection is a two way street. The earth and seas provide protection to us, giving us life-sustaining water, food, and oxygen, and we have human-made protections from the dangers of the sea, including foghorns, buoys that warn of reefs or rocks, lighthouses, anchors, lifeguards, the coast guard, sea walls and riprap to hold back the waves, and signage that warns of polluted beaches or dangerous surf.

Foghorns are a part of daily life in San Francisco, and many a foggy night I sleep with the window cracked open so that I can hear them. There is the regular tenor horn of Mile Rock lighthouse/foghorn in the strait, and the intermittent deep bass booming foghorns on the large cargo ships that pass in and out of the strait throughout the night. The sound of the foghorns is somehow comforting, evoking a visceral sense of protection. Joan Anderson, in *A Year by the Sea*, noted that during her first few months on Cape Cod, when she sat alone in her cabin one day feeling sorry for herself, the foghorns beckoned her to come forth to the beach, *"the depth of the howl guiding even the most hopelessly lost back to safety."* When she got to the beach, the fog was so dense that she could barely see the ground she was walking on. She had to rely on her other senses to navigate. On that foggy beach, she met an older woman who was to become an important friend and mentor in her life (someone she might describe as an "anchor"). The foghorn lead her to safety and lead her to a wise teacher, once she trusted herself enough to venture out in the fog. Beaches and rocky coastlines are dangerous places, but there is protection. Foghorns, buoys, and lighthouses guide the way through the perilous seas, if only we pay attention and trust in them.

We also have an obligation to protect the world around us from our own reckless behaviors. We can monitor our use of plastics and chemicals that pollute, and conserve water as much as possible. We can reduce our emissions and our carbon footprint in general, living as lightly on the land as possible. We can vow to leave no trace when we go to the beach or in the woods.

Resources

"Eskimos dwelling on remote, treeless Arctic islands for centuries constructed their homes from flotsam driftwood…Kayaks, too, were fashioned from driftwood frames upon which sea otter or seal hide was stretched taut. One-hundred percent organic ocean material went into the ancient's homes and conveyances. Coastal natives throughout the world depended on this early form of Home Depot delivered via Federal

Express—in this case, drifting currents—and so invested the oceans with a powerful 'gifting' reputation."
(Skye Moody, Washed Up, p. 17)

Life offers us many resources if we are open to receiving them. Some of those resources are external, like the flotsam used by indigenous people for centuries, and many are internal gifts and talents that we have developed over our lifetimes. Some of us are creative and quick-witted, others have incredible strength under stress, some are great communicators and can bring people together, some are visionary leaders, and yet others are powerful educators. Our combination of gifts and talents are unique. As I have reflected on my own gifts and talents in the past few years, I have given much thought to the concept of trust. Far too often, I have doubted my own abilities and that of others rather than trust.

Trust comes in two varieties, trust in self and trust in external circumstances and other people. Trust starts as an inside game. If we cannot trust our own inner voice, if we have doubts about our abilities, it is nearly impossible to trust in anyone else. We all have resources that we can tap into in times of need. We need to learn to trust the protections in our lives and rely on them to guide us. Our inner voice and deep wisdom typically knows the right course to take in any situation, if we trust our own instincts. Somewhere along life's journey, I had lost the ability to trust my own instincts. I had lost touch with my own inner wisdom because I overvalued the voices of others and let doubt overcome me.

Now, as I am reclaiming my own wisdom, reflection time on a beach gives me the time and place to access my own inner wisdom. In my work life and personal relationships, I can easily get caught up in the expectations of others and make decisions that are not always the best for me. I have learned that I am a slow processer if the exchange has any emotional component to it, and I often need to ask for time to think over some issue before I decide on an action. Snap decisions often do not come from my heart and gut, but only from racing thoughts. I still struggle with trusting my own decisions. The decision to move became easy when I had the epiphany on the beach, but in most situations, there is no sign, no lighthouse beacon to guide the way.

I also have some difficulty in trusting others, not surprising if I cannot fully trust myself. Life circumstances often cause us to doubt that we can trust others. For example, I am still trying to recover from a situation with a person that I thought I could trust with my life. This person did something that felt like such a betrayal to my trust, that it has taken me years to recover. How could I have been so wrong about this person? I had months of doubting my inner knowing. But with time, and reflection on the beach, I have realized that I cannot control or fully understand another person. It was not wrong of me to trust and love this person. Her "betrayal" does not mean that my heart was given to the wrong person or that I should not have loved and trusted her. I have learned that love is never the wrong choice, but with love comes the possibility of pain. I have to trust that I have an infinite capacity for love and compassion, and to give it freely. Trusting another person is an incredible act of vulnerability.

Healing

"When inward tenderness finds the secret hurt, Pain itself cracks the rock, and Ah! Let the soul emerge."
(Rumi)

A few years ago, I treated myself to a solitary writing retreat in a cabin on Tomales Bay in January, a time when Point Reyes National Seashore is virtually empty. I brought books on writing, writing paraphernalia, and a small bag of rocks that I found particularly comforting. I was struggling to let go of a romantic attachment that had a powerful hold on me. I thought I had found a soul mate, and I felt deeply that I was "meant to be" with this person, but the circumstances were all wrong. A relationship was not possible, but I had attached myself to the fantasy like a barnacle to a beach rock. Part of the purpose of my retreat was to write my way out of this attachment. I unpacked my stuff, explored the quaint little cabin and the grounds around it, and then decided to go to the grocery store a few miles down the road before I started writing. On my way to the grocery, I saw a little cottage festooned in Tibetan prayer flags, with smiling Buddhas of all sizes, and a variety of lawn ornaments occupying nearly every square inch of the yard. *Spirit Matters* read the sign outside. I entered and was immediately overwhelmed by the floor-to-ceiling displays of books, scarves, saris, drums, wall placards and posters, beads, incense, and so much more, all jammed into a tiny space.

I turned to the right and at my eye level on the greeting card rack, a beautiful card jumped out at me. The background color was in shades of rock-gray and steely gray, accentuating a picture of a rock against a foggy gray background. A rose bud with just a hint of pink blush emerged from the stone and the quote from Rumi that begins this section was printed inside. I immediately sensed that the answer to my attachment was in this card. Suddenly the allure of the store was gone. I bought the card and went back to the cabin, groceries forgotten. The card pulled it all together for me—the rock image symbolized the lump in my heart that was the pain of my unhealthy attachment, the rose bud emerging from the rock was a symbol of hope that the rock would crack open. The words of Rumi were healing, and combined with the beautiful visual image, helped me to see the lesson in this painful experience. I wrote furiously for an hour, and when I put the pen aside, I felt lighter than I had felt in months. I was not yet "healed" from the attachment—that would be a process of ups and downs, progress and back-sliding, but this moment of synchronicity of words and images from an external source provided the insights I needed to start the healing process. My love of rocks took on an even deeper meaning in terms of my own healing. Pain could split open the rock, and love would win. I learned to look for healing lessons in nature.

A few months later, another moment of synchronicity fostered even deeper healing from this attachment. I was in Chicago on a business trip and was catching up with an old friend that I had not seen for more than a year. She was the type of friend with whom I could fall into easy rapport regardless of time and distance. I told her of my frustration in giving up this attachment and how much I wanted to let go but could not, because, of course, one should never give up a soul mate. She pulled a book out of her backpack and told me that she has just finished reading it and knew that I would find it helpful. On the plane the next day, I started to read and ran across a passage that spoke to me in the same way that the Rumi greeting card had. The passage read:

"A true soulmate is probably the most important person you'll ever meet, because they tear down your walls and smack you awake. But to live with a soulmate forever? Nah. Too painful.

Soulmates, they come into your life just to reveal another layer of yourself to you, and then they leave." (Elizabeth Gilbert, Eat Pray Love)

How perfectly this captured my experience, and what a lesson it was. It led to another shift in perspective that fostered the healing process. I have learned that healing from emotional pain does not mean erasing the original feelings, but instead, seeing the lesson within the experience and integrating that lesson into my daily life. I may always love this person who felt like a soul mate, but I can transform that love into one with no expectations of the form our relationship should take. Indeed, we may never again have a personal relationship, but that does not diminish the value of the love and high regard I have for her. Love is good, being vulnerable and giving my heart to this person is good—what is not good is hanging on to expectations that the relationship will have a certain form or function.

Lighthouses are also a metaphor for protection, and for developing trust. The image of light, whether the high intensity illumination of a bright sun at midday or the more dim, mysterious light of the moon, or of light reflecting off of water, is often a symbol of acquiring inner knowledge. "Enlightenment" comes from the root word light. Being in the dark symbolizes the opposite—ignorance, lies, and lack of clarity. The lighthouse with its intense, regular beacon scanning the far horizon is a powerful symbol of hope, another important resource that keeps us alive.

Water is also a healing element. As Lena Lencek and Gordon Bosker noted, modern beach resorts were created first because physicians touted the medicinal aspects of sea bathing, and the romantic poets reinforced the spiritual and aesthetic dimensions of swimming in the sea. Watching waves rise and fall is also healing. Salt air, mineral baths, the sun, and the relaxation of the beach experience draw people who need healing. As we often turn to our mothers when we are sick or in pain, we also turn to the original mother of us all, the ocean, to heal from all that ails us. I find that beach walking is so much more healing and satisfying if I can remove my shoes and walk in the water. In Northern California, walking barefoot in the wake of the ocean has another advantage. The icy cold water wakes me up and brings me fully into the present moment!

According to Gaia theory, all life forms are physically connected to each other through the oceans, the air, fresh water, and the other fluids of the earth. All the elements are healing forces, readily available to us. Gaia, in contemporary theory, is not a deity per se, but a regulatory process that arose from millions of years of evolution. Deep ecology is a movement that values the diversity of all life forms on earth, and asserts that humans do not have the right to reduce this diversity, except for our survival. It is based on the principle that we place relationships, creativity, spirituality, and community over material goods, and use these principles in our daily conduct in business, government, and daily lives (Callenbach, *Ecology*). If we abide by these principles of interconnectedness, we recognize that we cannot heal ourselves (our inner or outer houses) without concern for the healing of all living things and the earth that sustains us.

Going Deeper
1. What images symbolize protection for you? For some it may be the beacon of the lighthouse sweeping the sea, or the anchor that holds the boat in place during the

storm. How can these images of protection be used in times of stress? Create a visual image, as detailed as possible, that you can retrieve whenever you need it.
2. What aspects of your self are completely trustworthy? What can you always rely on? Now look at parts of yourself that you have not always been able to trust—how can you shift your perspective or behavior toward greater trustworthiness?
3. Do you feel a deep sense of trust in your current relationships? If not, where and why is the trust lacking?
4. What kinds of nature experiences do you find to be the most healing? Is the feeling of healing the strongest at the sea, the mountains, the deserts, the forests, a riverbank? What about those settings help you heal? How can you bring those healing elements into your everyday life?

16
Detachment/Letting Go

"The beach was covered with beautiful shells, and I could not let one go by unnoticed. I couldn't even walk head up looking out to sea, for fear of missing something precious at my feet...One cannot collect all the beautiful shells on the beach. One can only collect a few and they are more beautiful if they are few."
(Anne Morrow Lindbergh, Gift from the Sea)

During my first four years of beachwise living, I often came home from beach walks with pockets weighed down by rocks. I spend much of my time on beaches like Anne Morrow Lindbergh; head down in awe of the beautiful variety of glistening rocks in the surf. My apartment became a rock shop with beach stones on every flat surface. I purchased a fish bowl so that I could submerge the ones that looked better wet. Soon I needed a second bowl, then a third one. I started placing rocks on the window ledge in my office. Finally one day, I reached saturation. I realized that I did not need to "own" the rocks--that I could enjoy them on the beach, but leave them behind for the next rock lover to delight over. I realized that letting go of material things was an ongoing process, and good practice for a deeper emotional and spiritual letting go. If I could observe and revel in the beauty of the rocks and shells on the beach, and then move on, I could also observe, enjoy, and let go of pieces of my ego. It seems like a small thing, but I have found it a useful small practice that helps me when I have bigger issues to let go of. And believe me, I have many bigger attachments to attend to! I am trying to picture those bigger issues like rocks that I might pick up and examine for a while, but then drop them back on the beach, skip them in the wake, or throw them as far as I can back into the sea.

Detachment and Wisdom

"This singing art is seafoam.
The graceful movements come from a pearl
Somewhere on the ocean floor.
Poems reach up like spindrift and the edge
Of driftwood along the beach, wanting!
Stop the words now.
Open the window in the center of your chest,
And let the spirits fly in and out." (Rumi)

Wisdom requires detachment and ability to stay open to many possible outcomes. Angeles Arrien, in *The Four-Fold Way*, defines detachment as *"the capacity to care deeply from an objective place."* We learn about detachment from our experiences with loss—the loss of personal attachments to people or things, loss of our own "turf," loss of structure or meaning in our lives, loss of good health, and loss of control. When we can recognize that we never really have control over anything except the way we feel, think or act on a situation, we can let go with some degree of acceptance, rather than bitterness or resignation.

Angeles noted that some indigenous cultures call on the ocean as the teacher of wisdom, as well as calling on ancestors for guidance. After all, the ocean is our ultimate ancestor, mother of all living beings. Indigenous cultures consider water as sacred because it cleanses, nourishes, heals, and purifies; it is fluid in its literal and figurative sense, able to flow over all obstacles, thus a good metaphor for flexibility, adaptability, and detachment. The current and the waves fling shells, rocks, driftwood, and seaweed upon the shore, and then sweep them away again, never hanging on to the material things. If I become too attached to a particular beach, because I like the rocks, or the way the sandy beach feels under my feet, I am sure to be disappointed the next time I visit the beach, because it will be different. Angeles (*Second Half of Life*) suggested that we have three layers of detachment to consider as part of our wisdom work: we must detach from material gain, from self-importance, and from the urge to control or dominate others.

Human pain and suffering comes from forming attachments. Suffering is intensified when our egos hold on to certain outcomes. How much greater ease would we have if we could let go of ego attachments? Nature helps us put our egos in perspective.

"We are partly drawn into the woods, to the ocean, and to lush green meadows, because the waves, trees, and grasses are free from egoist habits of grandiosity, deficiency, comparing or judging. They rest naturally in what they are, without self-consciousness, merged within the seamless fabric of life." (Mark Coleman, *Awake in the Wild*, p. 121)

When attachments become obsessive and rule our lives, we call them addictions. An addiction is characterized by intense craving and a feeling that only by having this thing that I want, can I be happy. We all have desires or simple wanting, and we can easily deal with them unless they turn into addictions, which are characterized by physical or emotional dependency and unbearable cravings. We can crave things, people, or ideas, like craving to be a certain kind of person, or craving to be romantically involved with a certain person. We can also crave to be wise, which ironically, interferes with developing true wisdom. Craving leads to fear, jealousy, envy, depression, and anger. It is in the gap between what we crave and what we have where the suffering is experienced.

People are prone to many kinds of addictions beyond those that we normally think about, such as addiction to food, gambling, sex, alcohol, tobacco, or drugs. We can also become addicted to drama, perfection, and a need to know (Angeles Arrien, *The Four Fold Way*). If we get attached to drama in relationships, if we get "high" on the excitement and chaos created by drama, our relationships will suffer. If we get addicted to perfection, our work may suffer, because the work is never "good enough." If we get too attached to the need to know, we may not be able to make decisions, because we will never know enough. The addictions all become excuses to stay in our comfort zone and not stretch and grow.

In our current technologically-dominated world, it is easy to get addicted to our screens. We obsessively text, tweet, facebook, or instagram, and we get all of our news on our devices. We watch Youtube videos of cute cats and doting dogs, play games, and email. Our devices have become a major cause of insomnia and are rewiring our brains to a more shallow way of accessing knowledge. When we search for information online, we tend to read only a few paragraphs of any website before clicking to the next link. We may not take the time to check the veracity of our sources, and we jump from idea to idea with no logical connection between them, except for a search term. We rarely engage with ideas in a deep, meaningful way. We must learn to use this incredible technology for the gifts that it can bring us, but prevent it from overtaking our lives. How often have you witnessed couples or families out to dinner, every individual on their device rather than engaging with the people sitting next to them?

Letting Go

"Walk slowly now, small soul, by the edge of the water. Choose carefully all you are going to lose, though any of it would do." (Jane Hirschfield)

Ego and identity get all mixed up for me. I have a sense of who I am though my identities, which stem from my cultural upbringing. That societal indoctrination forces me to think of myself as a woman in my 60s, a professor, a lesbian, white, a progressive, and a writer, among other identities. These identities are then maintained both by outside forces (when someone yells "dyke" out a car window or a student greets me with "hello, professor"), and by my ego. My ego attaches qualities to my identities that can result in pride, envy, greed, judgments, arrogance, doubt, shame, and a host of other thoughts/feelings that create the delusion of separation from others and from nature. Ego keeps me trapped in thinking that I am a unique, special individual, different from all others. I think these identities that I created to define myself or that were assigned to me by my culture, are grasped onto by the ego and hinder my growth and development as a spiritual being. Identities are the roles I play; they do not define me. Ego represents my unhealthy ways of coping with life; it does not define me either. I have to shed some aspects of both identities and ego to find myself.

Angeles Arrien (*Yearlong Indepth*) noted that giving up unhealthy ego processes does not mean neglecting the self—our egos allow us to survive in our cultures. She promotes walking "the middle path" finding the balance between ego superiority and self-denigration. The middle way is to nurture the body, honoring it as the only vessel we will have in this life. The middle way honors our connection to the sea, earth, and all things, and keeps our egos in check or in balance. We need enough ego to feel confident in our abilities, but not so much as to cause arrogance, or too little to result in self doubt.

As Mark Coleman noted, if we can look beyond our egos, we will have more energy to reach out to others and act for the benefit of others and for nature. There is no "other" and no "us versus them" in reality, as we are all part of the same whole. I know that the ultimate goal is to give up the notion of a separate self altogether, but I'm not ready for that step yet. In the meantime, I will work on giving up unhealthy ego processes and defenses and focus on walking the middle path.

Letting go of regrets is one of my daily struggles. I have spent too much precious time on this earth fretting about some past event. I have particularly deep regrets about losing connection with a very dear friend, the one I considered a soul mate. My regrets center on the actions that co-created an unhealthy dynamic after it was clear that we would not have a romantic relationship. I was so desperate to hang on to the closeness that we had developed, that I became clingy and dependent and drove my cherished friend away. I was too intense to be around. I recognized these behaviors as they were happening, but seemed powerless at the time to change my actions. My ego was in control, not my authentic self.

The point is, the situation is over, long in the past, but my regrets still cause me pain. I have not fully let go of the attachment, and the suffering prevents me from shifting my perspective and truly letting go. What do I fear will happen if I really let go of this attachment? Why am I still holding on to it? Somehow, letting go feels like being unfaithful to this heartfelt connection. I know it's irrational, but I think I fear never feeling this type of deep connection with another person, so I hang on to my side of the attachment, even though it's only a fantasy now. How warped is that? The situation reminds me that thinking alone does not alter one's behavior. I can see on an intellectual level that my attachment is irrational, unhealthy and causes me pain, but I have not addressed the deeper heart and gut connections. My connection to this person was a mind, body, and soul experience, so addressing it only at the level of the mind will never be successful.

Giving up the ego attachment starts with reducing the craving. Roger Walsh (*Essential Spirituality*) provides guidance on doing just that. He said that the first step is to recognize that suffering is feedback—it signals an attachment. Sometimes, just that awareness is enough to shift my perspective. The next step is to stay open to the experience of craving—what does it feel like? Paying attention to it, and noticing that it is transient may help. If necessary, I can reflect on the costs of the craving—what consequences has it had on my life? How much needless suffering have I caused myself? Finally, I can look at the beliefs that underlie the craving. What do I think I get from this attachment? Does it make me feel superior; does it make me special? Something powerful is causing me to hang on to the attachment; otherwise I would have let it go long ago.

Maybe my hanging on to attachments to people, identities, or ideas is related ultimately to my fear of death. Death is the ultimate letting go, as we release our physical form. As we ascended from the sea to live on land, giving up our gills and fins, we will eventually transcend the earth as well, giving up our bodies. Until that final letting go, we can practice letting go of the thoughts and behaviors that harm us, and others, and strive for a healthy detachment. For now, I'll keep practicing with the rocks—maybe giving up the harder attachments to people and things will continue to get easier.

Going Deeper
1. Make a list of five concrete things that you would like to "let go" such as guilt about a specific action you took or did not take, resentments toward specific people, judgments about a person or situation, or attachments to people or things. Select one item on the list, generate ideas about how to begin the process of letting go, and try to find the reasons why you are holding on to this attachment—what do you get out of the attachment? Imagine how your life would be different if you did let go. Now use the same process to evaluate the other items on your list.
2. In what ways do your social identities, or the roles you play at work, in the broader society, in your family and relationships, interfere with being your authentic self? What aspects of identity are you willing and able to give up?
3. Here is a meditation practice adapted from Mark Coleman (*Awake in the Wild*), called "Paying Attention." I will locate the practice on the beach:

Find a quiet, secluded spot to sit on the beach, and study the oncoming waves. Let go of everything you know about waves, your memories, associations, knowledge of tides and wind, and so on, and simply experience the waves with all of your senses. Imagine how the wave might feel—wet, cold, silky, refreshing; hear how it sounds without trying to describe the sound; see how the light of the day shines upon it, or how the colors change as the wave crests and breaks; breathe deeply and note how it smells; salty, fishy, like seaweed. Stay with the sensory experience for as long as you can. At first, it may be only 2 minutes, but with practice, you can extend this meditation practice in paying attention.

Letting go of thought and experiencing the world through the senses is a powerful practice toward wisdom.

17
Clarity, Confusion, and Fog

"What release to write so that one forgets oneself, forgets one's companion, forgets where one is or what one is going to do next—to be drenched in work as one is drenched in sleep or the sea."
(Anne Morrow Lindbergh, Gift from the Sea, p. 100-101)

In this book, I have tried to distill those moments of clarity I experienced on the beach into words. In my beachcombing of literature, I have mined the gems of wisdom from other writers, much wiser than myself. During the process of writing the book, I have had many moments that mirror Anne Morrow Lindbergh's experience of being "drenched in work." But there have also been moments when the task felt difficult, maybe even impossible. Some truths can be condensed into nuggets of gold, as shown by the many beautiful quotations sprinkled throughout the book. These statements touched my soul because they expressed some emotion, some sensation, or some truth that I have experienced myself—the truth shines through the words because of clarity. I have always been drawn to aphorism—those pithy little statements that contain such depth of meaning. Truth-tellers waste no breath on useless words—they speak clearly, from the heart, with no embellishments or drama. We recognize the truth when they speak. Here are some examples of aphorisms—do you feel "truth" in them?

> *You cannot teach a crab to walk straight. (Aristophanes)*
> *Nature does nothing uselessly. (Unknown)*
> *By three methods we may learn wisdom: First, by reflection, which is noblest; Second, by imitation, which is easiest; and third by experience, which is the bitterest. (Confucius)*
> *The environment is everything that isn't me. (Albert Einstein)*
> *A journey of a thousand miles must begin with a single step. (Lao Tzu)*
> *All art is but imitation of nature. (Seneca)*
> *A ship in harbour is safe, but that is not what ships are built for. (William Shedd)*
> *Anyone can hold the helm when the sea is calm. (Publius Syrus)*
> *Darkness reigns at the foot of the lighthouse. (Japanese Proverb)*
> *In a calm sea every man is a pilot. (Spanish Proverb)*
> *Fear is the little darkroom where negatives are developed. (Mark Pritchard)*

Oh, to be able to condense wisdom this way, into a golden nugget. Many of these authors were inspired by the sea, and remind us that all lessons to be learned exist already in nature. Sometimes clarity comes only from a change in perspective. We become accustomed to a certain way of viewing the world and miss all the rest. When we shift perspective, we see the world with new eyes. In writing about tides on the Long Island Sound, Mary Parker Buckles (*Margins*) wrote:

> "*Being a landlubber, I watched land shrink and swell when I went to the shore. I didn't see water rise and fall. The Sound has slowly changed me. Now I focus on the liquid. Its margins slop onto mainland and island stones like lapdogs that rush a vacant sofa. They leap. They're not allowed to stay.*" (p. 270)

Buckles wrote about how frustrating it was to write about tides, as the margins of land and sea constantly change. Words are concrete and fixed; tides are not. Clarity in writing comes from being able to pin something down and describe it so that others can have the same experience. But words can never really capture the subtlety and texture of true wisdom. Wisdom is like the ocean—dynamic, immense, deep, fluid, and life-sustaining. We can only view glimpses of it from the shore, but we cannot experience it in its entirety.

Many types of wisdom are better felt than spoken. How do we express the depth of joy and even bliss when the world seems totally alive and connected? How can we explain those flashes of insight or peak experiences that arise unexpectedly and totally alter our thinking? Some authors write of body wisdom, intuition, or other forms of knowing that are not located in our brains with its extensive language system, thus cannot be easily described in words. Others talk of the emotions evoked by music that also activates some other parts of our brains or souls than the language centers.

Elizabeth Baskin (*Beach Wisdom*) hints at this; that beach wisdom comes from our hearts and is related to concepts like faith, or believing something in spite of a lack of concrete evidence for our logical minds to latch onto.

> *"the beach is a place where we rediscover our own wisdom. There we'll be, walking along on the sand...and suddenly, whom should we bump into but our own highest selves, dishing out all kinds of wisdom we forgot we knew. That's what the beach does. It gives us a chance to hear the truths our own hearts whisper and to slow our careening inner pace to something that more closely matches the ancient rhythms of the tides...Faith also washes up. We watch the tide come in and the tide go out, just as it has for all the many generations before us. Perhaps the gift of the tides is to help us hold more faith in the ebb and flow of our own shifting fortunes or the rise and fall of our own careers or even the waxing and waning of our loves." (p. v)*

Clarity is more than just a cognitive or language function, and is related to a deeper sense of knowing that causes our heads, hearts, and gut to come into alignment.

Getting Clear

"Cold dark deep and absolutely clear,
Element bearable to no mortal." (Elizabeth Bishop)

So much in our lives contributes to lack of clarity. We are bombarded daily by messages in the media about what we should want, how we should dress, what and where we should eat, what kind of relationships we should be having, and how our bodies should look. In our jobs, employers or coworkers expect us to act in a certain way. Our families have expectations that they have conveyed to us in many ways over the years, so much so that we sometimes cannot distinguish our own wishes from those of our family. We strive to feel connected, so we sometimes give in to expectations of others, such as family, friends, media, or communities, but the cost of giving in is that we lose a little bit of ourselves each time. Each loss of our true nature raises doubt and confusion. No wonder we are sometimes perplexed by the question, "What do *you* want?"

Clarity comes from learning to access one's deeper knowledge and wisdom. Somewhere in there in our hearts, minds, and guts, we know what we want, but sometimes we have to shed several layers of external influence before we can get to it. As Candace Pert (*Molecules of Emotion*) taught us, knowledge is not only in our brains, but distributed throughout the body, with clusters around the heart and in the guts. This knowledge is accessed via emotions and sensory experience. To be truly wise and speak with clarity, we have to align the mind, body, and spirit and use all of our inner and outer resources.

Angeles Arrien (*Yearlong Indepth*) teaches that if something is clear to us, we will feel it ring true in our heads, hearts, and belly. Clarity is like the sound of a bell. If it is only clear in my mind (I think that I have "thought it through"), but I feel a twinge in my heart or a lurch in my stomach, I know the answer is not correct. When water is clear, we can see to the sandy bottom and spot any hazards. If the water is murky, to move forward might mean to step on a jellyfish or step in a deep hole. Clarity leads to right action. If we are not clear about the next step, then we need to wait for clarity to come before we take any action. Patience is a skill we need to access when we are not clear about an issue. If we take actions before we have clarity, we often make bad choices.

Fog: Blessing or Curse?

"Begin with the most distinctive aspect of the Bay Region climate—the diverse forms of fog. Traditionally, fog of any kind is a grim nuisance that seems to come from nowhere, hides the sun, obscures the terrain, and casts a damp pall over the land. Familiar with the murk that in their times darkened the streets of London, Shakespeare, Dickens, and many other writers associated fog with lurking evil. Combined with smoke, it creates the noxious urban miasma of smog. Dictionaries also identify "foggy" with vagueness, confusion, and other negative qualities." (Harold Gilliam, Weather of the San Francisco Bay Region, p. 1)

As Harold Gilliam pointed out, so often we associate fog with negative qualities or even evil. It is considered the opposite of clarity. We San Franciscans often complain about the summer fog—the "June gloom." But what about the positive aspects of fog? One early evening my first summer in San Francisco, I went to a party high on a hill in the Castro, sitting on a deck facing the north. To the right was the downtown skyline, to the left, Twin Peaks, a large hill that dominates the center of the city, and in between, the lower Castro neighborhood spread before us. As we chatted, I noticed a very thin ridge of white appear on the crest of Twin Peaks. In the next few minutes, it thickened and a wall of white vapor began to pour over the edge, following the contour of the hill. It was like watching a waterfall in slow motion. Still sitting in the sunshine, I watched in fascination as this fog flowed like water into the valley below filling all the lower dips and valleys, and then began to creep up the hill upon which I was sitting. When the fog reached us, first in thin wisps and tendrils of moist air, the temperature began to plummet. To the right, the city skyline still gleamed in sunlight for a few more minutes until the leading edge of fog passed over us and obscured the view completely. This was one of my first lessons in the microclimates of San Francisco, and the first of many days spent observing the varieties of fog with amazement. I watched fog roll, creep, infiltrate, or blanket a neighborhood, descending from above, rising from ground level, or blowing straight ahead softening the tops of the trees. Sometimes in the early evening, isolated wisps of vapor float down the streets of my neighborhood like ghostly apparitions.

Fog is one of the many things I love about San Francisco. It keeps the temperature mild, the city lush and green, and it has its own distinct beauty. It mutes the sounds of the city. I love to walk in Golden Gate Park in the fog, because the brilliant colors of flowers, and the wide variation in the shades of green of tree and foliage are accentuated by the gloom in the air. The majestic redwoods thrive because of fog and would perish without it. Strolling through Muir Woods in the fog feels like an expedition to an alien planet. The lessons of fog are many. Sometimes we need periods to cool down and contemplate the situation before moving to action. Confusion results when the truth is obscured—that confusion is a sign that we need to wait until the fog lifts before we take an action. In a dense fog, we have to slow down because visibility is more limited. We are more careful. Fog comes in a variety of forms and densities, engulfing the city for a few minutes or for days, much like our confusion about how to proceed in a relationship or how to make a decision about our careers. Fog is the message from nature to slow down and consider our options or responses.

If we consider fog as a positive gift from the sea, as nature writer John Smeaton wrote a century ago, we can explore the benefits of fog.

"the fog of the night, lifting but not passing off all day, afforded a delightful temperature, with restful tones of color. It is so that I best love the sea. Its grandeur, its significance, its solemnity, are felt far more than 'neath the all revealing sun,' and the water itself, deeply, darkly clear, seems more aqueous and elemental."

(J. Smeaton Chase, 1913, from Steven Gilbar, Editor, Natural State)

Sometimes fog is dense, nearly obliterating the outer world, leaving the city in a misty, silent, private world. But most of the time, fog is as Chase described it. It turns the world into grayscale: softer and more nuanced than in the brilliant sunlight. Ironically, sometimes visibility is better in fog than in bright sunlight. Fog does not blind you or cause you to squint like the sun does. Fog highlights the mystery, cools the temper, and opens a door to reflection. If we stop to listen and watch, there will be guidance. Fog is conducive to reflection and deeper thought. Foghorns and lighthouses will guide the way, or our deeper internal senses will take over for our faulty and limited outer sense of vision. If I were a poet, I think I'd write an ode to fog!

Going Deeper
1. Take an issue in your own life on which you need clarity, and do a walking meditation on the beach for guidance. Set the problem in your mind as you begin, ask for clarity, and then focus on moving slowly and deliberately, feeling your feet sink into the sand, and noticing the quality of the air. Let your ideas flow. If you cannot physically go to the beach, visualize one as you walk outdoors.
2. Think about your own attitudes about fog. Do you find it beautiful and mysterious, a nuisance, or a potential danger?
3. What does this say about your relationship to clarity and confusion? Are you able to stay within uncertainty and confusion for as long as it takes to find the right answer, or do you tend to jump prematurely to an action or judgment to get out of the internal fog?

18
Spaciousness and Timelessness

"I find myself mostly lowering my habitual gaze-out-to-sea and settling down to rummage in these greenish-brown, often stinking, bug-infested wrack lines, the likes of which I must have skirted or stepped over thousands of times in my younger-me rush to get to the water…The wrack line, after all, is not some hieroglyphic the gods leave twice a day for us to decipher…we're doomed it seems, to try to make meaning…the least we can do is try to figure out how to look at what's here—all these small things that the sea, arriving like an empty handed guest, nevertheless keeps handing out as gifts. I don't know yet how, if at all, these objects are connected, what kind of coherence they might suggest." (Barbara Hurd, Walking the Wrack Line, p. 7)

In my mind, place/space and time go together and they both relate to perspective and context. Each present moment is set in a specific place. We often associate particular emotions with places where some significant event occurred. Ask people in the baby boomer age group where they were when JFK was assassinated—most can tell you in sharp detail where they were and what they were doing when they got the news. Younger people may have the same clarity about where they were and what they were doing at the time of the news of the September 11, 2001 terrorist attacks. I suspect that election day of 2016, will be emblazoned in the memories of many people as well. Those of us concerned about climate change, human rights, and reducing the materialism/consumerism in our society consider this election potentially disastrous.

Perspective shifts over time, and reframes our memories as we integrate new experiences. The quote from Barbara Hurd that starts this chapter explicitly addresses that change in perspective. Perhaps the "gaze-out-to-sea" perspective is one of the future, and the focusing on the wrack line is a perspective of present moment and immediate space. I, too, find that gazing out to sea can be too daunting. I feel safe to view the horizon where the sea stretches to infinity when I am safely in my apartment—the picture that begins this chapter is the view from my living room. But when I'm on the beach, it is harder to look to the horizon for any length of time unless I have some specific purpose, such as watching for whales. The Pacific Ocean is so vast that my mind cannot take it in fully, so I lower my gaze to the edge of the water and focus on the concrete, nearby experiences of rocks, swash, and shells. Instead of the wrack line, I walk the "rock line" seeking stones that symbolize my connection with both earth and sea. If this rock can survive multiple tumbling in the sea, maybe I can survive the toils of life and end up on a beautiful beach somewhere, shiny and smooth. I rarely feel as alive and present in any aspect of life as I feel when walking alone on a beach.

Space

"Though I deeply appreciate the wildness of faraway places, the feeling is more diffuse and metaphorical than the special affection I have for Bay Area experiences that mirror those of my youth. For example, if I walk up to a local crag I climbed as a teenager, my hands naturally grab just the right ledges and cracks in the rock…Similarly, my eyes flow easily across even the most complex Bay Area landscapes in a way that satisfies my soul. (Galen Rowell, Bay Area Wild, p. 59)

What determines why some spaces become home and others do not? Some authors define home as the place where they grew up, the places they experienced as children, like Galen Rowell, in the quote above. He re-discovered the wonder of his own backyard after years of photographing distant exotic locations. Like strangers to the Bay Area, as an adult he tended to think of the region in terms of cable cars, ferry boats, and the well-manicured Golden Gate Park, until he and his wife flew over the Marin Headlands one day and marveled at the amount of wild lands they saw. Jane Hollister Wheelwright, talking about the California coast ranch where she grew up, said, *"the coastline of the ranch is like the floorplan of my life"* (The Long Shore, p. 92).

Others (me included) learn to appreciate a very new and different geography as home, such as Mary Parker Buckles, in *Margins*, who in her adulthood went from "landlubber" to beachcomber, or Barbara Gates, in *Already Home*, who described her attempts to make her house in Berkeley into "home" by studying the history of her house and the neighborhood. Most of us feel a need to call someplace "home," yet we define that feeling of home in different ways.

Angeles was fond of asking groups to share "what is the land that shaped you?" This experience taught me a lot about myself. Growing up on the plains, I experienced the "wide-open" sensation of sky. From my backyard as a child, I could clearly see sunrises and sunsets over the flat terrain. Miles of cornfields rippled in the wind, interrupted occasionally by grazing cattle or hog farms and tangled green rows of low-growing soybeans. I grew up in a town of 200 people and had the run of the county. I would join my friends on bicycle on summer mornings and we would range from stream to ditch to wooded groves along the gravel country roads all day long. My summer days were spent out doors. As an adult, I discovered gardening as a way to re-connect to nature, and had my first brief glimpses of bliss when I thrust my hands into the dark rich Midwestern dirt.

When I moved to San Francisco, I lived in temporary housing for the first eight months in a noisy urban valley (Haight Ashbury). While I loved exploring the neighborhood, this apartment and neighborhood did not feel like home. When I found three temporary part-time jobs and decided to move for good, I started apartment hunting. After a few weeks of finding great apartments in bad locations, or lousy apartments in great locations, I found my home on a hill on the west side. I have never made such an important decision so quickly as the decision to rent this apartment. I soon realized that it felt like home because of the expansiveness of the view. Like my home on the plains, I could see big sky (and big ocean rather than a cornfield!) from my window. After ten years, I still sometimes feel like I'm at a vacation resort when I look out my window. I found the familiar in my new unfamiliar surroundings to link my original home to my new home.

When I meet new people, they often seemed surprised that I have so quickly adapted to San Francisco after a half century in a small town in the Midwest. I attribute my rapid acclimation to the epiphany I had on the beach that made the coastline feel instantly "at home." In my mind, I was always a beach bum, temporarily placed in the middle of the country to learn some important lessons before I came home to the sea. I am now equally comfortable in my new home and my old Midwestern terrain. When I return to the Midwest for visits, I do revel in the familiar landscapes and they bring back many happy memories.

Time (and Tide)

"In a sense, we are all flotsam and jetsam. Created in watery media, we wash up without personal choice on life's foreign shores, only to navigate unpredictable currents and tides, blown from one circumstance to another, until we land, finally, for the last time, eventually bereft of flesh and humors…like flotsam, our personal journeys will never be fully understood or explained. And thank the gods for that, for the journey is who we are; without our personal mystery and its individual transformations and permutations, we'd be as indistinguishable as grains of sand viewed by the naked eye." (Skye Moody, Washed Up)

We measure our life journey in linear time, as if that structure of time gives us more control over our lives. We have entire industries built on time—watchmakers, self-help books, daily planners and organizers, kitchen timers, and personal time-management coaches. We spend an enormous part of our youth wishing for time to speed up, and much of our adulthood trying to slow it down. In reality, we bob along life like the flotsam in the sea with little control over anything, including time. Life proceeds, the journey progresses, whether we feel ready or not.

A few years ago, I stopped wearing a watch. This has been a liberating experience. Of course, I cannot totally escape the demands of time and timeliness, and there are reminders of time all around me—the hours that I work at a computer, I have access to the time in the lower right corner continually. There are clocks in my home, office, and classrooms. I carry a cell phone that can function as a clock when needed. But on my personal time and at least twice a week, I go into nature without a watch or cell phone, and let my deeper wisdom tell me when to go home, find some food, or transition to another activity. This exercise is beginning to shift my perspectives on time.

The years of burnout that I experienced were characterized by a restlessness that was both mental and physical (and spiritual as well, although I did not recognize it as such at the time). I had trouble staying still. I often took long walks in parks or by the river or lake, but my mind was racing, jumping from one worry to another, or one uncompleted task or another. I had a fear of "wasting time." My midlife crisis was partly about feeling that I had less time ahead of me than behind me, and I was anxious about it. Giving up the watch has helped me to restore my body's rhythm and increase the amount of time that I'm "being" instead of doing. Mark Coleman shared in his book, *Awake in the Wild*, a Spanish proverb that says, *"How beautiful it is to do nothing and then rest afterwards."* I'm trying to take that philosophy to heart, and the lesson has to do with my perspective on time.

Another irony of our contemporary culture is that we value the products of doing over the processes of being. We sacrifice valuable time we could spend in nature and solitude to "accomplish things," when our accomplishments could be made more profound and meaningful by devoting time to deep reflection and integration. I know that my own teaching and scholarship have improved immensely since I started spending quality time on the beach. I am not more knowledgeable about specific facts of the topics I teach or write about, but I'm a deeper thinker and approach the processes of teaching and writing with more mindfulness, more focus, a broader perspective, and from a more grounded place. I actually accomplish a lot more tasks, and with a higher quality of work, when I take plenty of time off for reflection and integration.

Recently I was reading a text on Buddhist psychology, about the notion of nothingness and emptiness. I despaired to think that I had another phase before me. I was just getting comfortable with the shift from doing to being, and now I was forced to think about "not being!" This idea of the void or the vast emptiness that is timeless and place-less is terrifying to me. I find it incredible that many people actively seek out that place. I guess I'm still firmly attached to time and place. If I could be assured that my next life would be spent strolling on an ocean beach, I'd be happy!

As I reviewed my first draft of this section on time, the phrase "devoting time" struck me. This expression illustrates how much we revere time. The word devotion is generally associated with religion or spiritual practice. Perhaps we should reflect on ways to use our time in a sacred manner, rather than making time itself sacred. Time is a human concept. We decided how to mark the passing of time into years, months, days, minutes, and even milliseconds. Spending time in nature helps us to return to "natural" time, not dictated by the clock. The day starts when the sun rises and the night starts when it sets. We eat when our bodies tell us that we are hungry, not when the clock says it is dinner time. We rest when our body signals that it is tired, not when the cuckoo announces that it is bedtime. I have also used the phrase "spend time" implying that it is a commodity like money (think also of "save time"). This notion, too, binds us to a social construct of time as limited and precious. In some senses, of course, it is limited, but we have more control over how we perceive time than we think, and more opportunities to engage with time in a different way.

I have also realized that I need transitions in my everyday life—those few moments of precious time in the space between events to shift my body, mind, and spirit from one activity to the next. I always arrive at places early, another trait I got from my father. My childhood memories are filled with the sound of his voice on Sunday mornings, urging us to "hurry up or we'll be late." Quite to the contrary, we were always the first to arrive at church, to sit in the back right pew of the sanctuary, all by ourselves. I wonder now if Dad needed the time to transition from the hustle and bustle of getting seven children ready for church, to the quiet contemplation of a religious service. Maybe he needed those extra ten or fifteen minutes of silence to prepare to receive the message. I don't know. I never thought to ask him why he had this compulsion to be early.

But I do understand why I continue his tradition. I arrive at movies, talks, lectures, group sessions, plays and performances early enough to orient myself and select the best placement. Do I want to activate my right brain or my left brain? Do I want to blend into the background, or be up front and center and be noticed? I need to adjust to the new place and absorb its feel, clear my mind of whatever clutter I enter with, and open to the new event. This time for mental and physical preparation is critical to my wellbeing. I often have nightmares about finding myself somewhere totally unprepared. I am in front of a classroom with no notes and no clue as to the topic. Or I am a student, arriving to take a test for which I have not studied. I am out in public naked, with no knowledge of where to find my clothing. These dreams reinforce my need to build in time for transition and preparation. Being unprepared makes me feel vulnerable. In this case, a short amount of time for preparation and transition saves me much anxiety later. I'm starting to think that this transition time for me is similar to what people seek in meditation; a time of transition or calm between the thoughts. I look for the same thing between activities to ground myself.

Going Deeper
1. Describe the land that shaped you. How did it contribute to the person you are today?
2. Do you feel at home in your current space and location? If not, what activities could help you develop the comforting sensation of being home?
3. How do you use your time? Are you treating time as sacred, or considering the things you produce as more valuable? How could you alter your perception or use of time?
4. Mark Coleman (*Awake in the Wild, p. 23*) suggests a meditation for cultivating spacious awareness. Find a place with an uninterrupted view of sky or ocean (or both). Sit or lie down and take in the vista, gazing from side to side to take in the 180 degree view, putting the sky and sea in front of and around you. Let your awareness expand to merge with the spacious view, letting your thoughts float away like clouds.

19
Balance

"In Brittany men say that if a person lies with his head against the beach sand, without even looking up he can tell which is the third wave. It comes in more powerful, wetter, fiercer than the rest, and it has the loudest roar on the coast. In Scotland, they say that three waves come in succession that are violent and strong and then one that is soft and gentle. The ninth wave is a frightening wave in many parts of the world. But in Wales, people say that the ninth wave is a particularly beautiful wave that belonged to the daughter of the sea." (Robert and Seon Manley, Beaches: Their lives, legends, and lore, p. 10)

Balance is about finding and maintaining one's center, and staying in the formidable middle. Balance is equilibrium, and it depends on identifying one's own patterns and the regularities in the outside world. How nice it would be if we could always count on the ninth wave being a beautiful blessing from the sea. Complete balance and predictability, is, of course, an illusion, much like the tides. Tides are always coming or going, and only for a split second is the tide at its highest or lowest point. Instead, water is constantly in motion. So are our bodies, thoughts, feelings, and the world around us. The key to balance is to recognize when our movement strays too far from the middle ground, and to correct our course before too much damage is done. We have to be vigilant to all the influences around us, and to our responses to these events—to keep our head to the beach sand to detect the patterns of incoming waves of emotion. If one area of our life is "out of whack" it has repercussions for all other parts of our being. In our search for balance, we try to find regularity in the world around us, which allows us to predict what might happen next, but the world is often not predictable.

After reading the passage about the regularity of waves, the next time I sat on Baker Beach, I spent an hour counting and classifying waves. My first system was to rate each incoming breaker by its size—small, medium, or large. I started counting with a very large one that shook the ground beneath me, and filled the air with salty spray. I noted it in my notebook: L for large. It was followed by two more large waves, and then a small one, LLLS, and Aha!, there was a three wave pattern, my mind said jubilantly. But then came another small one, and then a medium one, a large one, and a small one. Soon my notebook had this notation: LLLSMLSMMMSLLSMSS. Woops, I had jumped to a conclusion based on way too little data, hoping (expecting) to see a three-wave pattern. I started to pay closer attention. I looked not only at the size (which I had measured only by my sketchy estimate of the height of the wave), but also how high up the beach the wave flowed after breaking. To my surprise, the biggest waves were not necessarily the ones that came up the highest. Sometimes a small wave surged higher up the beach before breaking. Wave action was related to height, speed, volume, length of time between swells, and probably lots of other factors that I could not detect with my puny human senses. Some waves broke in long regular patterns—the crest would start to spill over at one point and break uniformly down the line for 50 to 100 feet. Others crested and flowed over in short 5-10 foot segments. Some waves crested 10 feet from the edge of the water, others 40 feet away. Sometimes two waves would be cresting at the same time—one close to the edge and the other farther out. Other waves started to crest in two places and flowed together until the two crests met in the middle, splashing up in the air and dissipating the wave. I noticed that the waves were bigger a few minutes after a large cargo ship had silently steamed past on its way under the bridge. Some waves, regardless of their height, churned up the sand, and others spilled over crystal clear with little or no disturbance of the sand. And then there is the variation in color. One day I observed the effects of the red tide at a beach at Point Reyes. The waves were rolling in with deep blue swells, and then as they rose to crest, became golden as they spilled over and then pure white as they crashed. In other lights, the waves as they spill become an aqua green or gray. What amazing variety in a phenomenon that my mind had pegged as uniform and regular. My notion of balance was suddenly complicated. I knew I needed to become a much closer observer of my own thoughts and behaviors and the world around me if I was to stay within my center in the midst of all this complexity.

We have so many different, but interrelated body, mind, and spirit systems that staying in balance is a messy and complex business. I'll arbitrarily divide this chapter into physical, emotional, and spiritual balance, which are related to our individual selves, and then discuss balance with the outer world of nature/environment in the last section.

Physical Balance

"Beauty built on the edge of the beach—maybe everywhere?—is in part beautiful because it cannot endure."
(Barbara Hurd, Walking the Wrack Line, p. 30)

One of the lessons of aging that has been particularly hard for me is learning to adapt to an ever-changing body. Over the years, several factors have converged to affect my physical balance—both in the literal and figurative senses. I have intermittent vertigo, degenerative disk disorder, and joint stiffness. These factors can make me feel "tipsy." I have developed a fear of falling and a fear of heights—afraid that if I get off balance, I won't be able to right myself and I'll take a fall. Where I once loved to hike up steep trails and had no fears about scrabbling over rocks or walking out on a slippery tidal flat, now I often experience an emotional paralysis when faced with loose rock or a steep trail. I cannot make my body move, and end up backtracking to avoid twisting or falling. As a consequence, I have limited my walks to trails I know are relatively flat, and I often avoid new areas, because I fear falling and being left alone in the wilderness. When I feel the fears related to physical balance, my emotional and spiritual health might also go out of balance. I wish I could see the beauty in this fragile body and I wish I could accept its impermanence. Instead, I get afraid or deny my own limitations, or I am filled with regrets that I can no longer do things that came easily in my youth. Neither of these responses leads to balance and harmony.

Another struggle for me is about diet. There is so much temptation to eat badly, and I do love to eat. I use food to reward myself for a job well done, to commiserate disappointments, to socialize with friends, and to write. One of the joys of exploring San Francisco is sampling the wide variety of restaurants with foods that I never encountered in my life in the Midwest. Much of my writing is done in a booth in a diner-type restaurant, where I feel guilty commandeering a booth to myself unless I keep ordering food and drinks. I try to select healthy food, and to make choices that sustain and protect the environment as well, not always easy when I eat out so much, and not so easy when the "bad" food tastes so good! So how do I find balance when eating is such a central and enjoyable part of my life?

Stephanie Kaza (*Mindfully Green)* offers a plan she calls a "green practice path" that I am beginning to implement around my food choices. She sees healthy eating as a harm reduction strategy—one that is accomplished slowly and mindfully. She asked questions to help guide us in making better choices about food, such:

- What harm was done to animals or plants during the production of this food?
- What harm was done to the environment during the production of this food?
- What harm might be done to my health if I eat this food?
- What harm results from the transport of this food from where it was grown or produced to where I am?

For example, on rare occasions, I crave red meat. If I am mindful about this, I have to consider the abysmal condition of cattle farms and the inhumane overcrowding, the antibiotics and hormones injected into the cows, the conditions at the slaughterhouse, and the effects of manure run-off into the water system, which eventually gets into the ocean. I must think about the risks of cardiovascular disease and other health problems from the high fat meat, the gas emissions from transporting that meat across the country, and the type of packaging it comes in, among other factors. I may not choose to give up meat entirely, but I may choose to reduce the harm by eating it less often, in smaller portions, and choose locally grown and produced meats. I cannot totally avoid harm, because if I choose to eat, something must die. But I can be more mindful about it and eat only what I need from farms that use organic methods and have humane treatment of their animals. This takes careful observation and learning about local food options.

I have also found tracking my health to be useful. I keep a small notebook next to my bed and at night, I jot down everything I ate, how much and what kind of exercise I got, and how I felt physically and emotionally. The conscious effort of writing it down makes me more mindful of patterns and where I'm getting off track. A day or two of lapses is ok, but when I start to see I'm off track for three days in a row, I take actions the next day to get back into equilibrium. Walking on the beach regularly helps me to get in touch with my physical body. When I'm most attuned to the inner workings of my body, I can feel the effects of insufficient exercise or the bad food choices, and I can track my fears and emotions more easily as well.

Finally, there is the matter of sleep. I have found that a strong predictor of feeling irritable, off balance, and having negative thoughts is lack of sleep. There is so much stimulation in the typical day of a citizen of the United States, from traffic, to high-octane caffeine drinks, work and family demands, and television programming and advertising that act like they are on speed. Trying to relax to sleep can be a major challenge. I have found that my ability to slow down and relax at night is related to exercise, diet, amount of caffeine, and stimulating activities in the evening. If I honor the transition time I need, I will turn off the TV, computer, and telephones by 9 pm and devote the rest of the evening to meditative reading, quiet music, or journaling (but not about any "stories" that contain the stresses and dramas of daily life!).

Emotional Balance

"Human beings destroy the ecology at the same time as they destroy one another...Healing our society goes hand in hand with healing our personal, elemental connection with the phenomenal world." (Chogyam Trungpa)

All healing and all attempts to find balance are related: the physical, the emotional, the spiritual, and the environmental are one. Our emotional balance is dependent on the health of the world around us, as well as how we treat each other. I find emotions harder to track than what I eat or how much I exercise. Somehow in my youth, I developed some inner walls or blockades that separate me from my feelings. Maybe it was the stoic Scandinavian cultural upbringing of my family and community that encouraged me to stifle and repress emotions, or maybe it stemmed from my feeling different than others and knowing I had to hide that difference. Probably it was both things and more. The result is that I often feel "upset" but have difficulty grasping the actual emotion that underlies it. I'm always amazed by people who can say, "When you said X, I felt Y." They sound so certain. I know when I feel upset or when my emotional balance is disturbed, but is it anger, fear, guilt, regret, shame, disappointment, irritation, humiliation, sadness, fear of loss, fear of entrapment? Who knows? I can process some events for weeks and never truly understand my emotional response.

Menopause further complicated my abilities to track emotions. Sometimes during the height of my transition/midlife crisis, I would be on a peaceful walk, enjoying the scenery, and suddenly I was crying for no apparent reason. During this time, I was grieving the deaths of my father and sister-in-law, in a painful personal relationship, trying to figure out if I could move across the country, AND I was menopausal. What a confusing time that was—I felt emotionally off-balance for three years.

Now my biggest challenge in staying in emotional balance has to do with conflict avoidance. I have been trying for the past five years to change a lifelong pattern, and learn to deal quickly and directly with interpersonal conflict. Neither the "quick" nor the "direct" comes easily for me. I don't process emotional issues quickly and clearly, as I have mentioned before, so the best response in times of conflict does not come magically at the time of the conflict. I generally have the best answer about a day later and so often I have fervently wished to turn back time so that I could deliver just the right response at just the right time! Angeles Arrien proposes that we use a 24/3/7 rule about conflict or misunderstanding. It is best to address it in 24 hours, but if I am a slower processer (and I am), I probably need three days. If I cannot address the issue by seven days at the latest, then I have to let it go. I cannot blame the other person if I am the one who did not seek clarification or resolution of the conflict. This letting go of resentments caused by my own conflict avoidance is challenging for me. I am still seeking beach wisdom on this issue, but I find that the beach rock in my pocket, and knowing that I need time for reflection, helps me to ask for a day to think the issue over. I am trying to practice deep listening at the time of the conflict, reminding myself to refrain from judgments or any response until I have reached some level of clarity.

Spiritual Balance

"We tend to favor the notion that nature exists in a state of balance or equilibrium in which plants and animals keep their numbers pruned and in proportion. As if life were bent on consistency and selected for preserving the status quo. It's in our nature to see order and when we don't see it, to try to impose it." (Jennifer Ackerman, Notes from the Shore, p. 148)

I used to read about monks and wise elders and daily meditators with envy, imagining that they had learned the secret to spiritual balance—that they were serene and unruffled by anything that life could throw at them. I was dismayed to read further, to find out the human emotions and struggle that most wise people still experience. I yearned to have order in my life in all realms, but particularly in the spiritual arena.

The deaths of my father and sister-in-law threw me off balance on the spiritual plane (as well the emotional and physical dimensions). These events shook my sense of purpose and meaning in life. Watching my father decline rapidly in a matter of six months from a vibrant healthy 69 year old, to a frail 70 year old, brought the concept of human mortality and weakness to the forefront. My father had a good life, full of community service and stewardship, and he died with dignity and grace. I see that now, but at the time, his illness triggered my own fears of death and dying. I distracted myself from really dealing with these fears and from grieving for my father by falling into an unfulfilling and difficult relationship with a very needy person. In this relationship, I could feel needed; hence, my life had purpose, even though I could never really meet this person's needs. I now had a fulltime job trying to convince her that I was up to the task. She had extreme abandonment fears, so I appeased her by telling her I would never leave. When it became clear that the relationship was a disaster, how could I break my promise and end the relationship? I felt stuck. As a coping mechanism for my unmet needs, I started spending more time in my backyard and initiated an ambitious landscaping project that eventually took over the front yard as well. At first, it was a way to keep busy and not think, but very soon, it became a healing, spiritual practice to work alone in the yard. To avoid my needy partner being at my heels every moment, I started arising at 5 am in the spring and summer to work outside for a few hours before going to work. The physical labor, the solitude, and the deep connection with the earth as I dug, planted, weeded, built ponds and raised flower beds started to heal some of the pain of my losses, and kept me on an even keel even while in a difficult relationship. But I sunk into a despondent state in the winter when bitter cold, snow, and ice forced me indoors for the majority of the day with no escape from my partner's emotional demands. I lacked the courage to confront my partner, and was exhausted emotionally and spiritually.

When I moved to San Francisco, I was concerned about the loss of a yard and garden—could I survive without getting my hands in the dirt? The answer was yes. I replaced gardening, which was getting more and more difficult because of my lower back problems anyway, with beach walks and exploring the wilder areas of San Francisco. I remember one day in particular, about a year after the move. It was the middle of the week and I was walking on a deserted beach south of Half Moon Bay. It was warm, so I had shed my shoes and walked in a gentle cooling wake. The beach stretched ahead of me as far as I could see, pristine dun-colored sand with no rocks, no footprints, no seaweed—just miles of a narrow strip of sand between the ocean and the sandstone cliffs. I walked down that formidable middle between ocean and land and tears streamed down my cheeks. I felt totally alive and my spirit soared with the sea gulls. I learned that spiritual balance is closely linked with time in nature, particularly in solitude. I did not need my own garden anymore. That had nurtured me in the past, but now I got my sustenance elsewhere. What I had planted in my garden in Iowa, came to fruition and had been harvested.

David Richo (*How to be an Adult*) proposed that healthy maturation requires that we do both psychological work to bolster a healthy ego, and spiritual work to foster connection and serenity. The ego work focuses on integrating the shadow side, which he calls the neurotic ego, while enhancing the functional ego that helps us survive in the world. Spiritual work, such as meditation, creative expression, ritual, myth, storytelling, and imagery, puts the ego work in balance. I have found that walking or sitting meditation on the beach is one of my most powerful spiritual practices.

Balance and the Environment

"The prescription for healing the ocean is clear. The ebb and flow of tides, the growth of salt marshes, the consumption of little fish by big fish, and all the natural processes that make ecosystems work must be protected and restored to maintain ecological health." (Rod Fujita, Heal the Ocean, *p. 183)*

Rod Fujita has a number of concrete suggestions about healing the earth, most of which require policy change and systemic interventions. Books like his are helpful in understanding the big picture and knowing what environmental policies will have the greatest impact. Both he and Greenpeace point to overfishing as one of the most immediate threats to the ocean's health. More than one billion of the earth's population relies on fish as their major source of protein. Industrialization of fishing has decimated many fish species, polluted the ocean, and destroyed many ocean ecosystems by upsetting the natural balance.

Climate change is another critical factor—as the temperatures of the oceans rise, whales feeding grounds are being destroyed, diseases proliferate in the warmer waters, and coastal areas are threatened. In California, 80% of the population lives within 30 miles of the coast, creating an imbalance that taxes the lands resources. We are putting tremendous stress on the edge of our land and the seas, and must find solutions soon.

There are two floating garbage heaps in the Pacific Ocean each the size of Texas. Skye Moody (*Washed Up*) noted that a ten-mile area of this garbage dump consists almost entirely of plastic bags—they are labeled Taco Bell, Sears, Fred Meyers, signifying the brand consciousness of our culture. In the Atlantic Ocean, the Sargasso Sea is similarly littered with human debris. I am proud to live in a city that banned plastic bags and Styrofoam, mandates composting, and I commit to carrying a re-usable shopping bag. However, these individual efforts are not enough. I need to consider what my part is in achieving the larger changes in law that will reduce corporate polluting and plundering of the seas and land.

Stephanie Kaza (*Mindfully Green*) noted that U.S. household consumption continues to rise each year. We buy more cars, more TVs, more computers per household every year. As one individual, I have three computers, in addition to a smart phone. Do I really need that much technological connectivity? Mindfulness about what and how much we consume can help us to prioritize our purchases and reduce our burden on the earth and seas. Kaza noted that the $18 billion dollars per year spent on cosmetics could pay for reproductive healthcare for all women on the planet for a year. The $14 billion per year spent on ocean cruises could provide clean drinking water for everyone. Think about the personal energy needed for shopping—we must sort through hundreds of choices and we are exposed to about 3000 advertisements per day. Kaza suggested slowing down our consumer experience. In her classes, she asks students to make a list of everything they own. The experience helps students to see where they spend/consume unnecessarily. The next step is to think about where these things come from and how they are produced. This type of mindfulness underlies an ethic of environmental balance.

Going Deeper
1. What events or people put you off balance? How can you reduce or avoid these situations? If they are unavoidable, what can you do to restore your balance quickly?
2. Is there one area, physical, emotional, or spiritual, that is the most challenging for you at this time? Why?
3. What can you do as an individual to help restore the balance of nature? What two actions can you take this week?
4. Try Stephanie Kaza's suggestion to list everything you own or this is too daunting a task, choose one room of your home and list all the items in it. Which items are necessities versus luxuries you could do without? Which items are the most draining of natural resources?

20
Boundaries, Borders, and Margins

"Here is the fringey edge where elements meet and realms mingle, where time and eternity spatter each other with foam. The salt sea and the islands, molding and molding, roll upon rolling roll, don't quit, nor do winds end nor skies cease from spreading in curves." (Annie Dillard, Holy the Firm, p. 21)

What appears as a uniform strip of land when you first view the beach, actually has distinct (but overlapping) geological boundaries. The berm is the point where the highest waves reach. Beyond the berm, in the inland direction, is the backshore, the place of beach umbrellas, picnics, and sunbathers. The foreshore, toward the ocean, includes the intertidal zone, the space that is exposed or covered, according to the tide. That area varies widely as tides depend on the location of the moon and the sun and the season. The intertidal zone is bounded by the high tide mark and the low tide mark, which is different every day. Farther out to sea is the shore face, the underwater area varies from several feet to several miles in length, depending on the depth of the continental shelf. The shore face ends at the point where water can no longer move the gravel, sand, or sediment. In the case of sand, this is about 180 feet (Bosker & Lencek, *Beaches*).

These are not set boundaries, but flexible and fluid, as befits a beachwise philosophy. They are a reminder that boundaries are necessary and useful roadmaps, but should not be too rigid. Boundaries can only be drawn on still photos or maps. In real life, movement is constant and the borders constantly shift. Boundaries are socially negotiated and flexible. Ken Wilber often says, "the map is not the territory." Maps show us the outer edges or the typical margins of a thing, and some of what is contained inside and outside those margins, but do not tell us what is really there. That is left to us to explore and learn for ourselves.

Boundaries and Relationships

"The five Oceans of the world, Arctic, Atlantic, Indian, Pacific, and Southern, cover 70 percent of the surface of the earth…As easily identifiable distinct bodies in their own right, they are often thought of separately, however, they are really one group of interconnected water bodies which come together to form one continuous salt water entity." (Smithsonian Institute, Hidden Depths, p. 15)

Boundaries are critical in human relationships, because they permit separation and allow for each person to grow in his/her individual manner, but ultimately, we are all connected. How do we negotiate separation and connection in our relationships and set healthy boundaries? The poet Rilke proposed that healthy relationships consist of "two solitudes" that co-exist peacefully and support each other. Relationships, like the beach, are safer when they are conducted in the openness and safety of the backshore. The intertidal zone boundaries are too fluid and too constantly changing, leading to drama and chaos. The shoreface is underwater, leaving the relationship in the treacherous place of treading water, or worse yet, drowning. The key is knowing where the high tide line is, and staying above it. Of course, the backshore is not always a place of constancy and calm either, but from the higher vantage point, we can be on the lookout for high winds, big waves, oncoming fog, and shifting sands, and move before disaster befalls us. Being awake and mindful in our relationships helps us maintain healthy boundaries and avoid the ambiguous margins.

David Richo (*How to be an Adult*) provided a checklist for figuring out if we have healthy boundaries in our relationships. Some of the questions that I found helpful were: Do you have clear preferences and interests separate from your partner? Do you know what makes you happy and unhappy? Do you recognize your own moods as separate from your partner's moods? Do you have your own interests and hobbies? Is your relationship mutual? Do you say "no" when you do not want to do something? Do you respect your partner's boundaries? If the answer to many of these questions is no, you probably have blurred boundaries, and this can lead to serious relationship problems.

Angeles Arrien (*Indepth Yearlong*) noted that when boundaries are blurred in relationships, a dynamic of control and appeasement usually follows. One person imposes expectations on the other, which are perceived as controlling, and the other party either rebels against the expectations or gives in to keep the peace. This dynamic can lead to both individuals losing their essential selves, and creates a false self system about the relationship. The hard balancing act, according to Angeles, is to never lose sight of the fact that there is "my dream, your dream, and the relationship dream," and that they are all separate and valuable. So how do we keep living our own dreams while maintaining a relationship? I have often played the role of appeaser in relationships, giving in to the other person to avoid conflict. Every time that happened, a little more resentment would get stored in my memory banks until finally I would rebel. My partner, not seeing my carefully contained resentment (thanks to that great stoic Scandinavian upbringing I had), would be shocked or perplexed that I might be unhappy.

Boundary issues in relationships are often related to two underlying fears. The first is fear of loss or abandonment, which can lead to trampling boundaries and trying to desperately hold on to the other person. The second, fear of entrapment, can lead to fleeing the relationship if there is the slightest hint that the other person is trying to control or hang on too tightly—in this case, the boundary might become more like a castle wall with a moat full of great white sharks. Both types of fear can co-exist in one person, creating complex responses to other people, with the push and pull resulting from competing, irrational fears. The lesson of healthy detachment is critical to maintaining one's nature or essence in a relationship. Once we are attached to one particular outcome, we lose our flexibility and sense of humor, and the relationship suffers.

Boundaries between Self and Nature

"The edge of the sea is a strange and beautiful place. All through the long history of Earth it has been an area of unrest where waves have broken heavily against the land, where the tides have pressed forward over the continents, receded, and then returned. For no two successive days is the shoreline precisely the same...Always the edge of the sea remains an elusive and indefinable boundary." (Rachel Carson, The Edge of the Sea, p. 1)

Like the boundaries of the shoreline, another set of artificial, fictional borders mark the division of self and nature, self and others, and even the self-imposed boundaries within ourselves, such as thinking we have only so much time to give to someone, or only so much love to share. Sometimes we hoard our gifts and talents for ourselves, not wanting to share because we perceive them as limited resources, not limitless gifts. Some of the feelings of alienation and need for boundary setting stems from our separation from nature. As Lencek and Bosker (*Beaches: The History of Paradise on Earth*) noted, the beach could only become a place of spiritual renewal after society industrialized and became alienated from nature—that is, the split between culture and nature occurred. Spending time in reflection on a beach or other place in nature can restore our connection to nature and break down the false boundary of culture and nature. Culture is only possible because nature allowed humans to survive, evolve, and create culture. Culture arises from nature, but can also be used as a weapon to destroy nature, which will ultimately destroy culture as well. We can also create culture that protects and sustains nature. Culture is worldview, perspective, and mutable because it is all in our heads. Reconnecting with nature brings us closer to our essential selves, and closer to a harmony between culture and nature.

One of the boundaries that prevent me from connecting with nature fully is setting up expectations. As I neared the end of this book project, one sunny day in January I decided to go to Point Reyes for some whale-watching. I got to the observation point on the highest part of the hill by the lighthouse, and anxiously scanned the horizon. I secretly hoped to spot a whale before any of the other half dozen people up there. After ninety minutes with no whale in sight, I felt disappointed and retreated halfway down the hill to a bench overlooking the beach to eat a snack. A herd of elk or deer was grazing on the hill below me, hawks circled overhead, seals were pulled out at the end of the beach far below, and the sun was warm on my skin. As I absorbed the view and let go of what I thought I had come here to do—see a whale—I began to feel that deep connection with nature. My attachment to an outcome had been interfering with my ability to connect and to access my beach rhythm. I also recognized the shadow sides of my ego—competitiveness and pride (wanting to be the first to spot the whale) and my impatience had combined with my focus on the horizon to prevent me from seeing the rest of the view.

Getting Marginalized

"But no man moved Me--Till the Tide went past my simple shoe. (Emily Dickinson)

I have spent a lot of my life feeling like I lived in the margins of society. As a child, I recognized my same-sex attractions, but never felt safe revealing them to others. I had a lot of friends, but in many regards, they were a mystery to me, and I could not relate to them. I could not understand the joy they experienced playing "wedding," dressing up in their mother's clothes, or buying make-up. In the church of my family's choosing, I felt like an outsider. I did not believe what the others seemed to take on faith. I had questions, but did not know whether it was safe to ask them, so I didn't. At school, I was interested in intellectual endeavors and reading, unlike most of my classmates. I could not admit that I actually liked to study or they would thing me even stranger than they already did. The result of the marginalization as a child was that I built a thick brick wall between my real self and others to protect myself. But all it did was lead to alienation and a greater sense of separation. I realize now that I was protecting myself from my own fears of rejection, not any actual events.

Later as an adult, at times I felt my relationships were not validated, I nearly lost a job because of my sexual orientation, and I was harassed and threatened on a number of occasions by strangers. These events contributed to a feeling of "us versus them." I continue to feel on the outside at times, as I strive for more inclusivity in society. I don't want to marginalize any other persons as I have felt marginalized—I am committed to tearing down the walls, but often I don't know how to go about it. And I have to consider how I might have in the past and in my current life, marginalized others. Where have I imposed a border between me and someone else? Where have my actions led to the diminishing of some other humans, other living beings, or the earth?

What I have been learning about the margins since I began haunting California beaches is that it is important to carefully and mindfully learn the lay of the land. I carry tide tables in the glove compartment of my car, pay attention to weather forecasts, and I observe deserted beaches for signs of changing margins that might be dangerous. I try to view my surroundings with an ocean's view of margins—continually shifting. In life, sometimes I'm on the outside and sometimes I'm on the inside of that imaginary line. That line, being a fiction, can be re-drawn by conscious effort. But my careful study of beaches shows that some lines are too dangerous to broach, at least until I have more experience or more knowledge. Sometimes getting too close to other people can be dangerous, so I need to use my beach-honed sense of careful observation within human relationships and encounters as well as to monitor the tides and avoid stepping on jellyfish.

Going Deeper
1. Think of the people closest to you. Do you have firm and identifiable boundaries with these people? Do boundary issues affect your relationships?
2. Try writing a boundary contract with a significant other or family member. Provide a concrete roadmap of the margins and territories of this relationship. Use Angeles Arrien's idea of "my dream, your dream, and the relationship dream" to construct the boundaries of the relationship that are permeable enough to realize all three dreams.
3. In what aspects of your life have you felt on the outside? How have you dealt with feelings of marginalization? How have you contributed to marginalizing others or the earth?
4. What has been your experience with the fear of abandonment and the fear of entrapment? Do you have consistent patterns or different boundary issues in different relationships? How have these fears affected your intimate relationships?

21
Aquanimity

"Only when I allow my inner waters to ebb and flow in accordance with their own natural rhythm do I experience peace. Such equanimity modulates both deep pain and deep pleasures. There's nothing wrong with experiencing extreme emotional cycles (unless such cycles create needless suffering), but when storms threaten to overwhelm, it's useful to remember there's an alternative in the peace and steadiness of equanimity." (Robert Kull, Solititude, p. 290)

Robert Kull spent a year of solitude on a remote island in Patagonia, and struggled for months with finding a natural rhythm and learning patience. He sought to find equanimity, the ability to meet a disturbance without creating a disturbance (Angeles Arrien,

Indepth Yearlong). I had heard Angeles talk about equanimity on a number of occasions, but this time, it struck me differently. I had been at the beach that afternoon, collecting rocks and watching surfers. As I sat in circle that evening, I held a particularly smooth stone in my hand, turning it over and holding on to my beach experience. Then Angeles brought up the discussion of equanimity, and the new word, "aquanimity," came to my mind. I realized that hanging on to a beachwise experience in my everyday life strengthened this quality that I had learned from my parents. They both had reputations in the community as "unflappable," and "good in a crisis." They were kind, gentle, compassionate people whose presence was reassuring to others in difficult times. I knew now that some of that appearance of equanimity was their outer countenance—the Midwest stoic nature. But much of it was part of their natures—they had this quality of meeting a disturbance without creating a disturbance. I knew from feedback from others that I was perceived in a similar way, but that it had deepened in the years since I had moved and adopted my beachwise life. This was an unclaimed talent that I needed to own, so that I could strengthen it and use it more consciously in my work and relationships. Before I could totally own the gift, I needed to examine it more closely. I recognized that in my early adulthood, I had often resisted being like my parents in any way—not that I did not love and appreciate them, but I wanted a different kind of life, so unwittingly rejected much of their good qualities along with those I did not want to claim. Equanimity was one of those.

Equanimity

"I could never stay long enough on the shore, the tang of the untainted, fresh, and free salt air was like a cool, quieting thought." (Helen Keller)

As is my tendency when I encounter some new idea, I first did some reading on equanimity. The dictionary definitions were rather bland: mental calmness, composure, evenness of temper, especially in difficult situations. Equanimity refers to presence of mind and coolheadedness. The word comes from the Latin, having an even mind. One source I found suggested that equanimity was a quality extolled in many religious traditions and gave some examples:

- In Hinduism, the concept is related to Brahman, a concept of boundlessness, reality (as opposed to the world, which is unreal), and is that which is unchanging, pure awareness, and dissolves the mind and ego. In other words, equanimity is one's true nature.
- In yoga, equanimity is one of the four sublime attitudes along with loving kindness, compassion, and joy. It refers to a clear, disciplined, and balanced mind.
- In Buddhism, equanimity is one of four immeasurables. It is a steady, conscious realization of the transience of reality, and is ground for wisdom. It is described as abundant warm radiance of being.
- In Judaism, equanimity is the foundation for moral and spiritual development.

- In Christianity, Samuel Johnson called for evenness of mind, neither elated nor depressed, and equanimity is the necessary foundation for carrying out gentleness, contentment, temperance, and clarity.
- According to Islam, equanimity is the peace that comes from surrender and acceptance.

I think I liked Angeles Arrien's definition the best, although each religion brought a slightly different dimension to the idea. But I still needed some beach analogies to help me understand the nuances of the concept of equanimity so that I could personalize its applications in my own life.

Aquanimity

"Surfing's a more profound kind of sport than it looks. When you surf, you learn not to fight the power of nature, even if it gets violent." (Haruki Murakami, Kafka on the Shore)

Next I started reflecting on the wisdom of the beach to help me understand equanimity. Water is fluid and flexible, but incredibly strong. Being able to adapt to changing circumstances is not "wishy-washy" but a sign of strength. Waves are the epitome of transient, regular disturbances. A wave crests and spills over with incredible power, but the energy is absorbed back in the sea and the process starts over. When excess energy is absorbed, it does not disturb. The sea is in constant motion and change, with calm periods between waves; low tides give way to high tides and back again. There is no stability---like the surfer, we must constantly be vigilant to the changes in the wave to avoid getting too far off balance and tumbling over. This requires a cool head and an even temper. A surfer needs to become one with the wave, dissolving the separation between self and the wave. You cannot take the wind or the wave conditions personally, and get angry if the perfect wave does not materialize when you want it. Aquanimity is the process of staying present to what is happening, observing the conditions with detachment, and constantly making adjustments. I don't have to take on anyone else's emotional overflows, just acknowledge them or absorb them. I can use my energy wisely and model calmness and stay on my board.

So aquanimity encapsulated a beachwise definition of the experience of equanimity for me personally, and I could now apply the image of surfing through life, tracking the conditions of the wave and the wind and my own position on the board to stay centered and grounded. When I start to feel ruffled or disturbed by life events, I pack my metaphorical surfboard and head to the beach. To integrate this lesson, I created the poster that starts this chapter, bringing in concepts from Angeles Arrien's Fourfold Way as well. She works with four archetypes that are found in every culture in the world: Warrior, Teacher, Healer, and Visionary. In my picture, the warrior, who epitomizes leadership and right use of power, is symbolized by the power of water that can flow over any obstacle. The teacher, symbol of wisdom, has the capacity to go with the flow and adapt to nature's rhythms, not attaching to any particular outcome. The healer uses fluidity and flexibility as tools for healing work—making adjustments to stay centered on the board. Finally, the visionary is able to see the big picture and track all the conditions of the wave and keep the surfer on course. Visionaries are creative types and forward-thinkers.

Going Deeper
1. What does the term equanimity mean to you? Do any of the definitions in this chapter resonate with you?
2. What nature metaphors work best for you to help stay centered and calm in the midst of a crisis, conflict, or major change in your life?

22
Beachwise Wisdom as a Way of Life

"The multiplicity of the world will crowd in on me again with its false sense of values. Values weighed in quantity, not quality; in speed, not stillness; in noise, not silence; in words, not thoughts; in acquisitiveness, not beauty. How shall I resist the onslaught?" (Anne Morrow Lindbergh, Gift from the Sea, p. 119-120)

Anne Morrow Lindbergh titles her last chapter, *The beach at my back,* implying that we leave the beach behind once we leave the sandy shore. I do not believe that it must be so. Rather, we can live the life of the beach, and carry the beach in our pockets, our hearts, and in everything we do as long as we stay awake. As the bumper sticker notes: Life is a beach. That, I thought to myself, is how we resist the onslaught of daily living.

The beach is a teacher of unending wisdom, constant, yet always changing, and always at our disposal, given our connection to the sea—we come from the sea, our blood courses with the same salty mix as the ocean. Our hearts beat with the regularity of oncoming waves. We can carry the beach in our hearts, spirits, and our bodies into our work cubicles, crowded freeways, kid's soccer games, and high-rise apartment buildings. The ocean is part of our life cycle, or as Rachel Carson put it, *"For all at least return to the sea…it is the beginning and the end"* (*The Sea Around Us*). I submit that it can be our "middle" as well, if we allow ourselves to live out a beachwise wisdom. Henry Beston hinted at how we could accomplish this as he reflected on his year of living alone in a remote part of Cape Cod in the 1920s.

> *"My year upon the beach had come full circle; it was time to close my door…because I had known this outer and secret world, and had been able to live as I had lived, reverence and gratitude greater and deeper than ever possessed me. Sweeping every emotion else aside, and space and silence an instant closed together over life…It is as impossible to live without reverence as it is without joy… Do no dishonor to the earth, lest you dishonor the spirit of man…For all the gifts of life are the earth's and they are given to all, and they are the songs of birds at daybreak, Orion and the Bear, and dawn seen over ocean from the beach." (p. 216-218)*

So the key, according to Beston, is to cultivate gratitude and maintain a reverent attitude toward nature. This seems to me to be the keystone of the beachwise philosophy of life. Reverence for the blue earth means that we make a solemn and sacred promise to conserve and preserve the oceans and the earth in the same way that we care for our human loved ones. Gratitude must be a consistent practice, or we risk going back to sleep. Almost daily I encounter scenery or an event that causes me to pause and give thanks for my current life. Every time I return to the city after a brief absence, I draw a deep breath and give thanks that this is my home. Every time I set foot on a beach, I express my gratitude for its wisdom and honor the beach as a wise elder, my guardian ancestor spirit that guides my life. Whenever I can, I view sunset from the beach, watching the sun sink slowly below the horizon, seeming to drop into the ocean in a blaze of red, orange, yellow, and gold hues. I am slowly learning the variations of the seasons on the beach in my new home. Jennifer Ackerman (*Notes from the Shore*) noted that learning a new landscape takes time.

> *"Few of us have the privilege of living as adults in the place we lived in as children. Even fewer of us die where we were born…How many landscapes can fit inside the human heart? At first I felt disoriented here, as if I had been spun around blindfolded and set down reeling…A native landscape enters a child's mind through a meld of sensations; the smell of seaweed or hay, the sound of cicadas, the cold grit of stone. It is all heart and magic, confusion rather than order, but the feeling it evokes is wholly satisfying and lasting. Gaining this kind of deep familiarity with a landscape other than your native one is like learning to speak a foreign language. You can't hope for quick or easy fluency. You work from the outside in, by accumulating a vocabulary of observed details…slowly the strange becomes familiar and the familiar becomes precious." (p. 7-8)*

I truly feel privileged that I have had the opportunity to learn a new landscape in the second half of my life. It does not diminish the precious memories of cornfield, bean field, and rippling fields of hay; of woods, rivers, streams and lakes; of snow, ice, and summer humidity of my native Iowa. The learning of my new coastal landscape is from an adult's perspective, but is tinged with the childlike exploration and new discovery that engages "heart and magic." In fact, the beach has melted my jaded cynical adult heart and released the inner child to learn this new landscape through the senses. For me, the beach was always familiar in some deep archetypical way, and all the more precious for it.

Deepening a Beachwise Practice

"It is easy to become a spiritual dabbler. Instead of deepening our own contemplative practice, we take the easy way out and spend our time reading and thinking about what others have written. This can be extremely useful, but such teachings are only conceptual descriptions of someone else's insights and understandings; they are not a direct examination of the light and shadow of our own inner world." (Robert Kull, Solitude, p. 270)

Guilty as charged. I'm a spiritual dabbler. It has taken ten years of beach-going and intensive study of other people's writing and ideas to get me to see the value of trusting my own direct experience. I am only beginning to have a consistent, daily beachwise practice but I am already reaping the benefits. I am slowly developing my own unique theology and practice. I've dabbled and feel enriched by the dabbling, and now feel ready to deepen my practice by increasing the amount of time I contemplate my own direct experience.

Whereas Tom Hayden urges us to re-adopt an earth-based spirituality, I will belong to the sect that worships at the beach. I vividly remember my first communion in the Lutheran church in which I was raised. As the minister intoned the words of communion, I had a profound sense of "this is not for me." I never voiced those words until I left home, because the social life of a small rural town revolves around the church, and my parents were devout church-goers. For a long while as an adult, I rejected religion and spirituality, because I did not know there was a difference. When challenged to state what I believed, I usually shrugged and said, "The power of nature, I guess." It wasn't until I was nearly 50 that I really began to explore what that meant, and re-acquainted myself with my deep spiritual roots. My spiritual awakening began in the dark rich soil of Iowa, and is maturing in the cold, wet beach sands of northern California.

My spiritual roots ultimately take me to the shrine of my original birthplace to worship; to the beach. I believe that sacred wisdom is within each of us, as it is in the earth and sea that we come from. Wisdom arises from the integration of the inner and outer worlds that Angeles Arrien so wisely counseled. She often quoted a Native American saying, *"Be strong like mountain, fluid like water, warm like fire"* to remind us that nature metaphors contain the wisdom we need to regain our essential selves. If we map out the integration of the inner and outer worlds using Ken Wilber's four quadrant model as the framework, it provides a road map for living a beachwise life. He would call it integral life practice; Angeles called it integration work; others might call it a holistic approach—I think of it as my beachwise practice manual. My integral map consists of my intentions, and looks something like this:

My inner world of thoughts, feelings, personal development, and spirituality
- Use beach principles to stay in my integrity: be centered, grounded, clear, balanced, patient, and authentic.
- Work on the shadow qualities of my ego to reduce their effects, and enhance the more positive gifts and talents that I can bring forth to the world.
- Go to the beach at least once a week for reflection and integration of life lessons so I can keep growing and maturing.

- Stay awake.
- Cultivate curiosity and continue to learn.
- Foster my sense of humor and creative fire.
- Give gratitude every day.
- Be aware of how my roles and identities affect my ego.

My physical body and the physical earth
- Be mindful about what I eat, and drink.
- Exercise, preferably outdoors.
- Practice ecology in daily life (heal my inner and outer houses).
- Take my body (and mind and spirit) to the beach as much as possible to stay in my natural rhythm.
- Carry a beach rock in my pocket to physically remind myself of my connection to the beach.

My sociocultural world
- Practice beach principles in my relationships (practice with mindful intention).
- Be involved in my neighborhood and communities and advocate for ecological principles locally.
- Teach others what I have learned (be a steward).
- Continue to seek guidance from wise elders to keep me on the right path.
- Seek out and participate actively in learning communities to keep growing.

The broader world
- Stay informed about laws and policies that affect the oceans.
- Use my vote wisely.
- Join political advocacy groups that take positive actions to sustain earth and sea.
- Write books and articles to share this wisdom with a broader audience.

Final Words: Emerging from the Fog

"The changing light in San Francisco
Is none of your east coast light
None of your pearly light of Paris.
The light of San Francisco is a sea light,
An island light,
And the light of fog…
And in that vale of light the city drifts anchorless upon the ocean."
(Lawrence Ferlinghetti)

Fog is such a curious phenomenon. It appears regularly, but to my untrained eye, so unpredictably. One morning as I watched the sunrise from my window, high on a hill on the northwest corner of the city, the fog hugged the ground to the south in a broad, low band, perhaps a mile wide, extending from the ocean into the Sunset neighborhood and completely covering Golden Gate Park. The fog blanketed the houses from my view and softened the edges of the neighborhood. It flowed up the edge of Twin Peaks with its iconic and huge telecommunications tower on the peak emerging above the fog, the bottom half of the tower completely obscured. There also appeared to be a fluffy cloud of fog over the bay. Over the rest of the city, at least the part I could see from my window, the fog was high, looking like an overcast day. The morning sun lit the underside of the high fog to the east with pink and orange highlights. The long strip of sandy shoreline called Ocean Beach, the sacred place of my coming home epiphany, appeared as a narrow margin of beige sand between the highway and the frothy water. The sea was relatively calm and steely grey this particular morning, and I could distinguish the water's edge on the horizon from the sky, something that is not always possible because of the fog bank that so often hangs off shore. The street below me was quiet. Neighbors had placed their garbage cans on the curb. I noticed one knocked over with garbage strewn into the street, probably the work of the huge raccoons that stroll down the middle of the street at night.

I consulted the tide tables and deliberated about where I wanted to go that day. The night before, I had vowed to visit a park bordering San Pablo Bay, but today my heart told me, as it so often does, to go to an ocean beach. Sitting here in my window, anticipating spending time on a beautiful beach with its wind and waves, I felt my heart expand with joy and gratitude that I can gaze on the ocean every day, and tread the sands of a beach regularly. I looked back upon my midlife crisis or whatever it was with greater compassion and appreciation for all that I have learned, and for motivating me to move to the sea. I guess that crisis, the hardest ten years of my life so far, was the Gift from the Sea that Anne Morrow Lindbergh wrote about. For from it, I have begun to comprehend who I am and what my life is about. My life is simpler, more balanced, and happier than it has ever been. I know this is not the happy ending of my whole life story, but only one interlude in a life that will continue its journey toward wisdom. In gratitude to the precious book by Anne Morrow Lindbergh that was one of the sparks of creative fire that launched this book, I will give her the last word.

> *"The waves echo behind me. Patience—Faith—Openness is what the sea has to teach. Simplicity—Solitude—Intermittency…but there are other beaches to explore. There are more shells to find. This is only a beginning." (Anne Morrow Lindbergh, Gift from the Sea, p. 128)*

Works Cited

Ackerman, Jennifer (1995). *Notes from the shore.* NY: Viking Press.

Anderson, Joan (1999). *A year by the sea: Thoughts of an unfinished woman.* NY: Broadway Books.

Anderson, Joan (2004). *A walk on the beach.* NY: Broadway Books.

Arrien, Angeles (2005). *The second half of life.* Boulder, CO: Sounds True Press.

Arrien, Angeles (1993). *The four-fold way. Walking the paths of the warrior, healer, visionary, and teacher.* San Francisco, CA: HarperCollins.

Arrien, Angeles (2008). *Notes from Indepth Yearlong group.* Sausalito, CA.

Baskin, Elizabeth (2003). *Beach wisdom: Life lessons from the ocean.* Kansas City, KS: Andrews McMeel Publishing.

Beston, Henry (1928). *The outermost house.* NY: Henry Holt & Co.

Bosker, Gideon and Lencek, Lena (2000). *Beaches.* San Francisco, CA: Chronicle Books.

Buckles, Mary Parker (1997). *Margins: A naturalist meets Long Island Sound.* NY: North Point Press.

Callenbach, Ernest (1998). *Ecology.* Berkeley, CA: University of California Press.

Carson, Rachel (1955). *The edge of the sea*, Boston: Houghton Mifflin Company.

Carson, Rachel (1950). *The sea around us.* NY: Oxford University Press.

Carson, Rachel (1965). *The sense of wonder.* NY: Harper and Row.

Casey, Susan (2010). *The wave: In pursuit of rogues, freaks, and giants of the ocean.* NY: Doubleday.

Coleman, Mark (2006). *Awake in the wild: Mindfulness in nature as a path of self-discovery.* San Francisco, CA: Inner Ocean Publishing.

Dillard, Annie (1977). *Holy the firm.* San Francisco: HarperCollins.

Emoto, Masura (2004). *Hidden messages in water.* Hillsboro, OR: Beyond Words Pub.

Fujita, Rod (2003). *Heal the ocean: Solutions for saving our seas.* Gabriole Island, BC: New Society Publications

Gates, Barbara (2003). *Already home: A topography of spirit and place.* Boston: Shambhala Press.

Gilbar, Steven (Editor, 1998). *Natural state: A literary anthology of California nature writing.* Berkeley, CA: University of California Press.

Gilbert, Elizabeth (2006). *Eat pray love.* New York: Viking Press.

Gilliam, Harold (2002). *Weather of the San Francisco Bay region.* Berkeley, CA: University of California Press.

Greenberg, Gary (2008). *A grain of sand.* Minneapolis, MN: Voyager Press.

Hay, John (1969). *In defense of nature.* Iowa City, IA: University of Iowa Press.

Hayden, Tom (2007). *The lost gospel of the earth: A call for renewing nature, spirit, and politics.* NY: Ig Publishing.

Helvarg, David (2001). *Blue frontier: Saving America's living seas.* NY: Henry Holt & Co.

Hempton, Gordon (2009). *One square inch of silence: One man's search for natural silence in a noisy world.* NY: Free Press.

Highland, Chris, editor (2001). *Meditations of John Muir: Nature's temple.* Berkeley, CA: Wilderness Press.

Hurd, Barbara (2008). *Walking the wrack line: On tidal shifts and what remains.* Athens, CA: University of Georgia Press.

Kahn, Peter (2001). *The human relationship with nature*, MA: MIT Press.

Kaza, Stephanie, Editor (2005). *Hooked: Buddhist writings on greed, desire, and the urge to consume.* Boston: Shambhala Press.

Kaza, Stephanie (2008). *Mindfully green: A personal and spiritual guide to whole earth thinking.* Boston: Shambhala Press.

Krishnamurti, J. (2000). *All the marvelous earth.* Ojai, CA: Krishnamurti Foundation of America.

Kull, Robert (2008). *Solitude: Seeking nature in extremes.* Novato, CA: New World Library.

Krutch, Joseph (1954). *The voice of the desert.* NY: William Sloane Assoc.

Lencek, Lena & Bosker, Gordon (1998). *Beaches: A history of paradise on earth.* San Francisco: Chronicle Books.

Lindbergh, Anne Morrow (1955). *Gift from the sea: twentieth anniversary edition.* NY: Vintage Books.

Louv, Richard (2005). *Last child in the woods: Saving our children from nature-deficit disorder.* Chapel Hill, NC: Algonquin Books.

Macy, Joanna (2007). *World as lover, world as self.* Berkeley, CA: Parallax Press.

Manley, Robert and Manley, Seon (1968). *Beaches: their lives, legends, and lore.* Philadelphia: Thomas Nelson and Sons Ltd.

Matthiessen, Peter, Editor (2007). *Courage for the earth: Writers, scientists, and activists celebrate the life and writing of Rachel Carson.* NY: Houghton Mifflin, Co.

Moody, Skye (2006). *Washed up: the curious journeys of flotsam and jetsam.* Seattle, WA: Sasquatch Books.

Moore, Thomas (1994). *The care of the soul,* NY: Harper Paperbacks

Pert, Candace (1997). *Molecules of emotion.* NY: Scribner Press.

Plotkin, Bill (2008). *Nature and the human soul: Cultivating wholeness and community in a fragmented world.* Novato, CA: New World Library.

Rowell, Galen (1999). *Bay area wild.* Emeryville, CA: Mountain Light Press.

Roszak, Theodore (1979). *Person, Planet.* Garden City, NY: Anchor/Doubleday.

Schlitz, Marilyn, Vietan, Cassandra, and Amorok, Tina (2007). *Living deeply: The art and science of transformation in everyday life.* Oakland, CA: New Harbinger Press.

Smithsonian Institute (2007). *Hidden depths.* San Francisco: Harper Collins

Sternberg, Robert J. (1988). *The Triangle of Love: Intimacy, Passion, Commitment.* New York: Basic Books

Thoreau, Henry David (1906). *Writings of Henry David Thoreau.* Boston: Houghton-Mifflin.

Walsh, Roger (1999*). Essential spirituality: the 7 practices to awaken heart and mind.* NY: John Wiley & Sons.

Warber, Sara and Irvine, Katherine (2008). Nature and spirit. In Goleman, Daniel and others, *Measuring the immeasurable: The scientific case for spirituality.* Boulder, CO: Sounds True Press.

Wilber, Ken (2006) *Integral spirituality: A startling new role for religion in the modern and postmodern world,* Boston: Shambhala Press.

Wilber, Ken (2000). *Integral psychology: Consciousness, Spirit, Psychology, Therapy,* Boston: Shambhala Press.

Wilber, Ken (2007). *The integral vision.* Boston: Shambhala Press.

Postscript
Using This Book in Discussion Groups

Reading is a solitary activity, but most meaningful human life occurs in interactions with others. Many people get more value from the ideas contained in a book through discussion with others. This book can serve as a bridge for the exchange of ideas. True transformational change rarely comes from merely reading a book, although books are certainly a good way to introduce new concepts or different perspectives that may move a person to change. Most of the time, though, the change process is slow and ongoing, and happens in spurts and setbacks. Change requires strong intention, consistent practice, and support. A group of like-minded peers committed to changing their lives can benefit from forming discussion groups. Some of the advantages of forming book discussion groups is that group members can:

- ❖ Deepen and enhance the lessons suggested by the book through the process of group members discussing their interpretations of the concepts of patience, flexibility, detachment, and so on.
- ❖ Share their own unique experiences with each concept to demonstrate how they have dealt with challenges in life—the sharing of stories is a time-honored tool of all cultures, past and present.
- ❖ Witness each other. Stating one's intentions in front of a group can be a powerful experience that deepens the commitment to change. In addition, witnessing change in others is equally powerful, and gives us hope that we too can change.
- ❖ Establish a climate of accountability to each other. So much in our culture encourages dishonesty and development of a false self system. Group members can practice and model authenticity and integrity.
- ❖ Become a place to consciously and intentionally practice giving gratitude publicly and celebrating group member's progress surviving and thriving amidst life's challenges. Ritual and group support is key to marking our progress—we have lost many of the rituals used in earlier iterations of our culture to mark life transitions, so re-introducing them can be transformative.
- ❖ Become a form of collective spiritual practice for all the reasons listed above.

There are many options for forming discussion groups—a group can be as small and intimate as couples in relationship reading the book together, discussing their core values, and using the book to deepen the communication in their relationship, or as large as a class on personal development. The book can be used as part of an ongoing group formed around another purpose, such as a religious or spiritual development group, a self-help group, a book club, or a class focused on ecology or spirituality. I will discuss two options—a one-time discussion group or workshop, and an ongoing group of 7 to 22 weeks.

A One-Time Discussion Group/Workshop

I recommend that a minimum of three hours, but up to six hours, be allotted for a one-time discussion session. This option requires having at least one person to act as the organizer and group discussion leader. Some ideas for format include:

- The group discussion leader begins with a personally meaningful quotation or short reading from the book, followed by a five-minute silent meditation for the group to contemplate the quotation and set the mood for the discussion to follow. Silence and stillness allow the body, mind, and spirit to transition into a more "sacred" and natural space.

- Introductions of group members should focus on gifts and talents rather than social identities. The purpose of this is to keep ego and identities at bay. Ways to foster this different type of knowing of each other in group include:

    o "Hello, I am ____, and when I think of the beach, I think of _____."

    o "Hello, I am ____, and I am known by my friends to be _____." [list a quality that is your best asset; something you can always count on like patience, generosity, compassion, authenticity, creativity, and so on]

    o Form dyads for each person to share the origin of their name (first or last): What does the name mean, or who was I named after?

    o In dyads, have each person respond to the question, "What is the land that has most shaped you? What type of nature/geography made you the person you are today?"

    o Ask each person to state which chapter of the book they found to be the most personally relevant at the time they read it, and why (but limit to 2-3 minutes per person).

The rest of the time can be spent going through the chapters one at a time. Allow some time for unstructured open discussion of the chapter. Some of the deepest discussions may stem from how individuals react to the concepts presented in the chapters—one may have a very different experience of patience or equanimity than I did as author, and that is rich discussion. If there is ample time available, use the Going Deeper questions to prompt discussion in the whole group, or if there are more than 10 people, in groups of 3 or 4. Alternatively, the group discussion leader can ask the group which chapters they would like to focus on. Close with another quotation from the book and a final five-minute meditation.

An Ongoing Discussion Group

As I have noted in this book, transformative change can be facilitated by setting intentions, paying attention, consistent practice, and guidance. All of these things can be enhanced in ongoing small group settings. If you choose to form a group, it could be a short-term commitment, such as holding seven sessions and discussing three chapters at each session, or have more sessions, perhaps even going through the book one chapter at time. Whatever length of time you choose, here are some suggestions for getting the most out of an ongoing group.

At the first session:

- Set intentions. Ask each group member to state as clearly and specifically as possible what they want to get out of the group, and what they want to change in their personal lives.

- Establish group guidelines. Have a discussion about how the group will be facilitated, how you will deal with absences, how you will monitor participation (e.g., what you will do if certain people monopolize conversations), how to deal with confidentiality, and how to best respect each other's differences. Be clear that the group is about self-help and personal development, not therapy. One way to keep a group from lapsing into a therapy session is to use Angeles Arrien's concept of generative speaking. With this, you explicitly discuss how sharing painful stories can trigger painful memories for others, so that every member should consider some questions before they speak: will my contribution further the conversation, ask a question of clarification, give an example of how I applied this idea, or otherwise, move the conversation forward in a positive way? If my motive for speaking is to tell an old story, to get attention, or to get sympathy, I should consider not speaking at this time. This group is not designed to address those types of sharing. When sharing about a past experience, each person should provide enough context so that the listeners understand the situation, but not go into traumatic details or processing about the event. For example, it might be enough to say "I have a long history of competition with my sister" rather than share a ten-minute story about the pattern.

- Choose a format. You may decide to go through the book in the order the chapters appear, or each group member can choose chapters that they will facilitate and schedule them in whatever order people choose. Decide how long the sessions will be (60-90 minutes would probably work best), how often you will meet (weekly, biweekly, monthly), where you will meet, and when you will meet. Set a structure for the group, such as beginning and ending with a meditation or guided imagery, opening with a check-in, or whatever structures work best for the group.

- If possible, schedule beach visits as part of the group experience.

You may decide to continue the group after finishing the discussion of Blessings from the Beach by reading and discussing some of the other books highlighted here. I would strongly recommend:

> *Gift from the Sea* by Anne Morrow Lindbergh
> *The Second Half of Life* by Angeles Arrien
> *The Four Fold Way* by Angeles Arrien
> *Living Deeply* by Marilyn Schlitz, Cassandra Vieten, and Tina Amorok

Or if you liked this book you might also enjoy my workbook, *My Life as a Tree* (available on Amazon), for reviewing your past and current life using parts of the tree. This book was written as a way of reviewing your own life, using analogies from trees; the roots are the strong character traits you have that help ground you in life, the branches are the paths you have taken in life, the bark is an analogy for the ego protections you put up to shield you from the hardships of the world. Although a personal book, it might be fruitful to discuss your own journey through life with others.

In whatever way you find the beach book helpful, I wish you ample blessings from the beach, and my sincere encouragement for you to continue your own wisdom journey along the beach or other nature spot of your choice!

www.ingramcontent.com/pod-product-compliance
Lightning Source LLC
Chambersburg PA
CBHW041543220426
43665CB00002B/22